The Qualities of Literary Machine Translation

Held at Machine Translation Summit XVII

Dublin, Ireland
19 August 2019

ISBN: 978-1-5108-9251-4

Printed from e-media with permission by:

Curran Associates, Inc.
57 Morehouse Lane
Red Hook, NY 12571

Some format issues inherent in the e-media version may also appear in this print version.

Printed by Curran Associates, Inc. (2019)

For permission requests, please contact the Association for Computational Linguistics at the address below.

Association for Computational Linguistics
209 N. Eighth Street
Stroudsburg, Pennsylvania 18360

Phone: 1-570-476-8006
Fax: 1-570-476-0860

acl@aclweb.org

Additional copies of this publication are available from:

Curran Associates, Inc.
57 Morehouse Lane
Red Hook, NY 12571 USA
Phone: 845-758-0400
Fax: 845-758-2633
Email: curran@proceedings.com
Web: www.proceedings.com

Machine Translation Summit XVII

DUBLIN
MACHINE
TRANSLATION
SUMMIT 2019

The Qualities of Literary Machine Translation

19 August, 2019
Dublin, Ireland

The Qualities of Literary Machine Translation

19 August, 2019
Dublin, Ireland

Preface from the co-chairs of the workshop

The question of translation quality and how to define and measure it is one that has occupied a central position in both translation studies (TS) and machine translation (MT) since their respective geneses. TS has largely turned away from questions of absolute quality in recent years, towards a pluralistic notion that any translation produced by a human is a genuine reflection of that human's interpretation of the source text. With this reasoning in mind and lacking any generally agreed standard by which to judge translations, ascribing absolute or relative quality to such translations would be self-contradictory (Drugan 2013: 45). MT, however, cannot adopt the same stance with reference to its own outputs, since they are not the direct products of human interpretations, and so, can simply be inadequate or unacceptable to target readers. Nonetheless, a definable ideal of translation quality remains elusive (Way 2013).

As MT systems have developed, their use by professional translators and by end users bypassing human translators altogether has become more and more an accepted practice. However, this acceptance is only applicable to certain domains of texts. Literature has historically been held up as one domain in which machine translation and computer aided translation (CAT) are both of little or no use (Alcina 2008: 95).

The aim of this workshop is to ask whether literature really is off-limits to technology.

Of the twelve abstract submissions received for this workshop, ten (83.3%) were accepted for presentation after peer review by the workshop's Organizing Committee. Of these ten, six presenters opted also to formulate full articles, which are published in these proceedings. Of those which did not opt for full publication, only abstracts are reproduced here.

The submissions are vary widely in terms of language pairs, with as many as thirteen languages: Catalan, Dutch, English, German, Greek, Irish, Polish, Portuguese, Russian, Scottish Gaelic, Slovene, Spanish, and Turkish, analyzed from a variety of angles and taking in different issues as they pertain to the qualities of literary translations produced wholly or partly by machines.

The presenters who opted to provide full articles are:

- Kuzman, Vintar and Arčan, who examine productivity and output quality in the case of the poorly resourced and under-studied language pair of English and Slovene;

- Matusov̌, who looks at stories translated from English to German and Russian by NMT systems, proposing a new form of error evaluation specifically tailored to literary prose;

- Ó Murchú, who examines the issues related to post-editing literary translations produced by an ad-hoc hybrid machine translation system, with a focus on the time and effort required to bring the output to the standard required for publication;

- Şahin and Gürses, who consider the pertinent question of retranslation as it relates to NMT, asking whether and how NMT systems might be brought to bear on practicing literary translation professionals' work in order to improve productivity;

- Taivalkoski-Shilov, who points out an important feature of literary texts that has thus far been over-looked in our research into literary machine translation and which future models may need to cater for, that of free indirect discourse;

- Tezcan, Daems, and Macken, whose work is a case study of NMT used to translate Agatha Christie's The Mysterious Affair at Styles into Dutch, with a focus on error rates and stylistic differences between this NMT and the published human translation.

The presenters who did not opt to produce full articles are:

- Oliver, Toral, and Guerberof, who focus on bilingual ebooks as they relate to the training of NMT systems with the aim of increasing the number of ebooks available.
- Sklaviadis, Gong, and Crane, who bring NMT models and a wide range of lexical resources to bear on the translation of the Homeric Classics.
- Toral, Oliver, and Pau Ribas, who compare the outputs of literary translations produced with generalized NMT systems and those specifically tailored to literature.
- Zajdel, who compares the decision-making processes of human translators and NMT as they relate to the translation of metaphor in literary texts.

James Hadley, Maja Popović, Haithem Afli and Andy Way

Organizers

Workshop Chairs

James Hadley	ADAPT Centre, Dublin City University
Maja Popović	ADAPT Centre, Dublin City University
Haithem Afli	ADAPT Center, Cork Institute of Technology
Andy Way	ADAPT Centre, Dublin City University

Contents

InLéctor: Neural Machine Translation for the creation of bilingual ebooks

Antoni Oliver González
Universitat Oberta de Catalunya
aoliverg@uoc.edu

Antonio Toral
University of Groningen
A.Toral.Ruiz@rug.nl

Ana Guerberof
Dublin City University
ana.guerberof@dcu.ie

InLéctor is a collection of bilingual ebooks intended for helping people willing to read the original version of a novel. The reader can move from a sentence in the original to the corresponding sentence in the translated version with a click. This can be of great help to readers facing problems in difficult passages. To date we have published several books in English, French and Russian with translation into Spanish or Catalan. These bilingual ebooks are freely available (https://inlector.wordpress.com) in epub, mobi and html, so they can be read in almost any device. Until now, we have published books in the public domain with translation also in the public domain or, in some cases, with the translation rights donated to our collection. It is difficult to find novels in the public domain with translations also in the public domain and for this reason we have been able to publish a limited number of books.

In this paper we present the process of training such a literary-adapted neural machine translation (NMT) system from English to Catalan and its use to derive parallel ebooks. We also present the results of a survey conducted by a user group who have read a short history in this format, namely Arthur Conan Doyle's *The yellow face* in the bilingual English-Catalan version. Our hypothesis is that bilingual ebooks save time consulting dictionaries and make the whole reading experience more fluent.

The use of NMT systems can boost our InLéctor collection as we can now publish a large number of novels in the public domain. This also means that we can offer readers machine translated versions of books that have not been translated to date into their native language. We also plan to train NMT systems for other language pairs in order to increase the number of source and target languages in the InLéctor collection.

Embeddings for Literary NMT

Sophia Sklaviadis
Tufts University
Sophia.Sklavi-adis@tufts.edu

Bowen Gong
Tufts University
Bowen.Gong@tufts.edu

Gregory R. Crane
Tufts University
greg-ory.crane@tufts.edu

With c. 100 million surviving words produced over more than 2,000 years —conventionally c. 750 BCE through 1453 CE— classical Greek offers a significant literary corpus. Homer's Iliad and Odyssey are two of the oldest Greek texts (c. 750 BCE) with linguistic-literary connections to the preceding Sanskrit oral poetry (Nagy 1974), as well as to the later European literary traditions. Homer has been consistently translated from antiquity to the present. The enthusiasm with which scholars have translated Homer has resulted in a complex accumulation of parallel texts, ranging from Chinese to Persian and Hindi. In French, there are more than 20 different modern translations of the Odyssey. In Modern Greek, translations at different time periods reflect changes in a language continuous with Homer's, yet inaccessibly distant without training. This paper presents a preliminary application of state-of-the-art neural machine translation (NMT) to the texts of Homer. We focus on modeling a standard edition of the source texts and English translations. We compare the effect of static, pre-trained embeddings on a seq2seq NMT model. First, we report on fitting the NMT model itself without a static embedding layer. We then discuss a qualitative evaluation of embedding spaces based on the mood-tense morphological variation of Ancient Greek verbs. Finally, we summarize the effect on the seq2seq model of pre-trained static embeddings trained (i) only on the texts of Homer (c. 200,000 words), and (ii) on the canonical-GreekLit corpus (c. 10,000,000 words, https://github.com/PerseusDL).

References

Nagy, G., 1974. Comparative studies in Greek and Indic meter (Vol. 33). https://chs.harvard.edu/CHS/article/display/6448

Automatic and Human Evaluations of Neural Machine Translation on Novels

Antonio Toral
University of Groningen
A.Toral.Ruiz@rug.nl

Antoni Oliver González
Universitat Oberta de Catalunya
aoliverg@uoc.edu

Pau Ribas
Universitat Oberta de Catalunya
pribasba@uoc.edu

Recently, neural machine translation (NMT) has emerged as a new paradigm in MT, and has been shown to considerably improve the translation quality achieved, regardless of the language pair (Toral and Sánchez-Cartagena, 2017). In addition, compared to the translations produced by previous paradigms to MT, those by NMT are much more fluent (Bentivogli et al., 2016) and also less literal.

Due to the above, we deem it appropriate to evaluate NMT on a content type that has historically been considered particularly challenging for MT: literary texts. Specifically, we target novels for the English-to-Catalan language direction and consider different NMT systems: commercial offerings as well as in-house systems tailored to novels trained under the recurrent with attention architecture (Bahdanau et al., 2014) and with an attention-only approach, commonly referred to as Transformer (Vaswani et al., 2017). We conduct two evaluations:

- An automatic evaluation with BLEU (Papineni et al., 2002), the most widely-used automatic evaluation metric in MT, on a set of twelve widely-known novels (Toral and Way, 2018), including for example J. Joyce's Ulysses and J. K. Rowling's Harry Potter The Deathly Hallows . The results show that NMT systems, particularly Transformer, bring notable improvements in translation performance.
- A human evaluation, on a fragment of Arthur Conan Doyle's The yellow face. In this evaluation a human post-edition of the text has been performed, making the minimum changes for the target segments to be acceptable. After this postedition, the errors have been manually classified in several categories.

Both automatic and human evaluations show that specifically tailored systems using a literary corpus perform much better than general-purpose commercial systems. The quality levels obtained with the tailored systems are good enough to use the MT system in certain situations, as for example where a human translation of the work is not available or for the creation of reading aids.

Machine versus human: Comparing human and machine translations of metaphors in *The Picture of Dorian Gray*

Alicja Zajdel
Trinity Centre for Literary and Cultural Translation, Trinity College Dublin
zajdela@tcd.ie

Although the recent shift from statistical to neural machine translation (MT) systems has made MT a frequently used tool in the translation industry, specialists in literary translation remain sceptical of the usefulness of the technology for literature. This study puts MT to the test, by exploring its possibilities and limitations when translating literary texts rich in metaphorical language. It does this by comparing solutions used by Google Translate to translate metaphors in *The Picture of Dorian Gray*, with those used by human translators across three languages: Spanish, Portuguese and Polish. Using a parallel corpus, this study identifies patterns in the decision-making processes of both MT and human translators and evaluates how and to what extent they differ. Through analysis and visualisation of the collected data, the results of this study provide an opportunity to assess the current suitability of Google Translate for literary texts and may be useful in the programming of improved MT systems in the future.

Neural Machine Translation of Literary Texts from English to Slovene

Taja Kuzman
Department of Translation Studies
Faculty of Arts
University of Ljubljana
kuzman.taja@gmail.com

Špela Vintar
Department of Translation Studies
Faculty of Arts
University of Ljubljana
spela.vintar@ff.uni-lj.si

Mihael Arčan
Insight Centre for Data Analytics
Data Science Institute
NUI
Galway, Ireland
mihael.arcan@insight-centre.org

Abstract

Neural Machine Translation has shown promising performance in literary texts. Since literary machine translation has not yet been researched for the English-to-Slovene translation direction, this paper aims to fulfill this gap by presenting a comparison among bespoke NMT models, tailored to novels, and Google Neural Machine Translation. The translation models were evaluated by the BLEU and METEOR metrics, assessment of fluency and adequacy, and measurement of the post-editing effort. The findings show that all evaluated approaches resulted in an increase in translation productivity. The translation model tailored to a specific author outperformed the model trained on a more diverse literary corpus, based on all metrics except the scores for fluency. However, the translation model by Google still outperforms all bespoke models. The evaluation reveals a very low inter-rater agreement on fluency and adequacy, based on the kappa coefficient values, and significant discrepancies between post-editors. This suggests that these methods might not be reliable, which should be addressed in future studies.

1 Introduction

Recent years have seen the advent of Neural Machine Translation (NMT), which has shown promising performance in literary texts (Moorkens et al., 2018; Toral and Way, 2018). Most research on neural literary translation focused on the comparison of statistical and neural models, whereas this paper is one of the first to present a comparison exclusively among NMT models, specifically between models adapted to novels and the mixed-domain Google Neural Machine Translation (GNMT) system, exploring whether adaptation to literary text leads to better performance of NMT systems. This is also the first research paper that investigates literary machine translation (MT) from English to the highly inflected and under-resourced Slovene language. The models are evaluated both with automatic evaluation methodologies, more precisely the BLEU and the METEOR metrics, and human evaluation methods, i.e. an assessment of fluency and accuracy, a measurement of the temporal dimension of post-editing effort and error analysis. Since the neural models are evaluated by multiple evaluation methodologies, we are able to compare evaluation methods, and determine whether they are efficient.

Our hypotheses were that all models adapted to literary texts would yield better results than GNMT, based on automatic (hypothesis 1), as well as human evaluation (hypothesis 2), and that the model trained on out-of-domain parallel data and retrained on the novel *Practice Makes Perfect* (model 'Novel') would perform better than the model trained on out-of-domain parallel data and retrained on the corpus SPOOK (model 'SPOOK'), according to both automatic (hypothesis 3) and human evaluation (hypothesis 4).

2 Related work

2.1 Machine translation of Slovene

The Slovene language poses challenges for MT due to its morphological complexity for all word classes and the lack of resources. Moreover, it is highly inflected, and it has a free word order (Krek, 2012). Nevertheless, several MT systems have been built between English and Slovene in recent times. In 2002, the first Slovene commercial MT system called Presis was developed (Romih and Holozan, 2002). This rule-based machine translation system was later followed by other foreign commercial systems, such as Bing Translator, Google Translate, Yandex Translate and Tradukka (Hari, 2018).

Additional systems were developed as a part of research projects, such as a statistical machine translation (SMT) system for Slovene subtitles, built in the framework of the SUMAT project (Etchegoyhen et al., 2014). Arčan et al. (2016) developed a publicly available mixed-domain SMT system called Asistent for translation between English and South Slavic languages, i.e. Slovene, Croatian and Serbian.

First comparisons of the performance of SMT and NMT approaches between English and Slovene were conducted in 2018, where SMT methods still outperformed NMT (Arčan, 2018). The translation quality of the NMT system can, however, be improved, by the addition of a parallel corpus containing selected sentences and by the enlargement of the neural architecture. Research, conducted by Donaj and Sepesy Maučec (2018), yielded more promising results. It revealed that NMT approach outperformed SMT in both English-to-Slovene and Slovene-to-English translation directions. Regarding the performance of commercial NMT systems for the translation between English and Slovene, Vintar (2018) compared Google's SMT and NMT for translating scientific texts with special focus on terminology translation. According to the BLEU score, GNMT outperformed the statistical system for both translation directions, however not for the translation of terms. In another study Hari (2018) compared the quality of Slovene translations of the English subtitles for the movie *The Lord of the Rings*, generated by the Bing Translator, GNMT and Yandex Translate. He discovered that Bing Translator outperformed GNMT and Yandex Translate.

2.2 State-of-the-Art in MT of Literary text

Until recently, there has not been much interest in the Computational Linguistics community regarding MT of literary texts, as the predominant opinion was that MT systems could never be useful for translating this type of text. Some of the first experiments were conducted in 2010 when Genzel et al. (2010) translated poetry with SMT systems from French to English and Greene et al. (2010) from Italian to English, producing translations that obey meter and rhyming rules. Another piece of research on literary machine translation from French to English was carried out by Jones and Irvine (2013), who translated samples of French prose and poetry using general-domain MT systems. Besacier (2014) conducted a post-editing experiment on SMT of literary texts from English to French which revealed that post-editing a pre-translated literary text could be used instead of a translation from scratch, although it does not achieve the same level of quality.

Toral and Way (2015) researched SMT of literary texts from Spanish to Catalan and carried out a human evaluation of the SMT models used. The findings revealed that evaluators considered 60% of the segments to be of comparable quality to professional human translation. In 2018, the same authors developed English-to-Catalan SMT and NMT models, tailored to literary texts, and compared them based on automatic and human evaluation. Both methods showed that the NMT system performed better, resulting in an 11% relative improvement over the SMT system (Toral and Way, 2018). Moorkens et al. (2018) also compared SMT and NMT systems, adapted for the translation of literature from English to Catalan, measuring post-editing effort with six participants. The findings revealed that all participants post-edited the NMT most quickly and that translation from scratch proved to be the most time-consuming. Moreover, the NMT model produced more fluent and adequate translations than the SMT one.

2.3 Analysis of Evaluation Methods

As manual evaluation is time-consuming and expensive to perform, it is regarded to be more accurate than automatic evaluation. However, research conducted by Callison-Burch et al. (2007) revealed low inter-annotation agreement for the assessment of fluency and adequacy, calling this method into question. To determine the inter-annotator agreement, they calculated the kappa coefficient, which is the proportion of time two or more annotators assigned identical scores to the same segments. According to Landis and Koch (1977), result from 0.0 to 0.2 means slight agreement, 0.21 to 0.4 fair, 0.41 to 0.6 moderate, 0.61 to 0.8 substantial and a higher score than 0.8 means almost perfect agreement. Analysis performed by Callison-Burch et al. (2007) revealed that the inter-annotation agreement for assessing fluency and adequacy was merely fair.

3 Experimental setup

In this section, we give an overview of the training and test datasets used in our experiment. Then, we present NMT systems and give insights into evaluation methods.

3.1 Training and Test Data

Bespoke models were trained on in-domain parallel data, either on the *Slovene Translation Corpus* (SPOOK) or on a corpus, consisting of a novel *Practice Makes Perfect*, written by Julie James, and its translation. In addition to these corpora, some models were also trained on out-of-domain parallel data to increase the lexical coverage of the training corpus. The out-of-domain data was mostly obtained from the OPUS web site (Tiedemann, 2012), which offers various parallel corpora, including Europarl, DGT, EMEA, KDE and EBC.

The *Slovene Translation Corpus* (SPOOK), a multilingual cross-comparable corpus of original and translated texts, was built in the framework of the Slovene Translation Studies: Resources and Research national research project which ran from 2009 to 2012. The corpus contains parallel corpora of literary texts in English, French, Italian and German and their translations to Slovene, as well as some original Slovene literary texts (Vintar, 2013). In this experiment, we used an English subcorpus consisting of nine English novels and their Slovene translations, i.e. J.R.R. Tolkien's *Lord of the Rings: The Two Towers*, Dan Brown's *The Da Vinci Code*, Eoin Colfer's *The Supernaturalist*, Colin Dexter's *The way through the woods*, Mark Haddon's *The Curious Incident of the Dog in the Night-Time*, Doris Lessing's *The Fifth Child*, J. K. Rowling's *Harry Potter and the Half-Blood Prince* and *Harry Potter and the Deathly Hallows*, and Zadie Smith's *White Teeth*. In total, it contains around one million English tokens.

In addition to that, we built a parallel corpus, consisting of Julie James's romance novel *Practice Makes Perfect* and the Slovene translation *Osem let skomin*, produced by Irena Furlan. The corpus, built with the CAT tool MemoQ, consists of 7,000 segments and around 100,000 English tokens.

The test data was drawn from a similar corpus, consisting of a romance novel *Something about you* by Julie James, and its Slovene translation *Nekaj na tebi* by Irena Furlan. Thus, all models were tested on a novel by the same author and translated by the same translator as the novel on which our author-specific model *Novel* was trained. The dataset used for automatic evaluation consists of 2,547 segments and 41,054 English tokens. Since human evaluation is more time-consuming, participants in the experiment were given much shorter excerpts from the novel. Half of them were to post-edit and evaluate an excerpt *The Discovery of Body*, consisting of 16 sentences and 175 English words, and to translate from scratch an excerpt *The Interrogation*, containing 15 sentences and 174 words. For the other half the task was reversed: post-edit and evaluate the excerpt *The Interrogation* and translate the excerpt *The Discovery of Body*. For the purposes of error analysis, we analyzed MT outputs of these two excerpts and an excerpt from the beginning of the novel. The total length of the text that was analyzed is 929 words.

	Tokens		**Types**	
	English	**Slovene**	**English**	**Slovene**
Generic	62,067,541	5,1428,154	387,259	641,726
Spook	1,009,551	946,728	33,207	73,446
Practice	101,118	94,923	6,323	10,391
Something	41,054	39,014	3,895	6,215

Table 1. Statistics on datasets, used for training the neural translation models

3.2 MT systems

Google Neural Machine Translation is an NMT system, developed by Google in 2016. It supports 91 languages, including Slovene. Moreover, GNMT enables translation between language pairs never seen explicitly by the system, also known as "Zero-Shot Translation". GNTM learns from millions of examples, which is made possible by Google's machine learning toolkit TensorFlow and Tensor Processing Units (TPUs) (Schuster et al., 2016; Le and Schuster, 2016). Google's current Universal Transformer NMT system is based on the standard Transformer, which is based on a self-attention mechanism and was found to outperform recurrent and convolutional models for English-to-German and English-to-French translation directions (Uszkoreit, 2017). In contrast to RNN-based approaches, the Universal Transformer processes all symbols at the same time and refines its interpretation by processing every symbol in parallel over multiple recurrent processing steps while making use of self-attention mechanism and devoting more attention to ambiguous words (Gouws and Dehghani, 2018).

Bespoke NMT models were trained using OpenNMT (Klein et al., 2017), a generic deep learning framework mainly specialized in sequence-to-sequence modelling. To improve the lexical coverage of out-of-vocabulary compound words, our NMT models were trained on sub-word units (Byte Pair Encoding). Initially, we used the default OpenNMT parameters, i.e. 2 layers, 500 hidden bidirectional Long Short-Term Memory (LSTM) units, 500 nodes, input feeding enabled, batch size of 64, 0.3 dropout probability and a dynamic learning rate decay. The networks were trained for 13 epochs. Then we also conducted some experiments by enlarging the neural architecture to 4 layers, 600 and 1,000 hidden LSTM units, and 600 and 1,000 nodes. As the results showed that the enlargement of the network did not have a large impact on the translation quality and that in some cases resulted in a decrease of the translation quality, we continued the training of the models with the default OpenNMT parameters. Similarly, experiments in which we trained the networks for up to 50 epochs did not result in the improvement of the translation quality, so we resumed the training of all models for 13 epochs.

In addition to GNMT and the generic NMT model (the baseline), trained on out-of-domain data, we evaluated multiple bespoke models, tailored to literature:

- model, trained on the corpus SPOOK (model 'Just SPOOK')
- model, trained on the novel *Practice Makes Perfect* (model 'Just Novel')
- model, trained on out-of-domain data and retrained on the corpus SPOOK (model 'SPOOK')
- model, trained on out-of-domain data and retrained on the novel *Practice Makes Perfect* (model 'Novel')
- model, trained on out-of-domain data and retrained on the corpus SPOOK and the novel *Practice Makes Perfect* (model 'SPOOK + Novel')

3.3 Evaluation

Firstly, all models were evaluated based on automatic evaluation methodologies. Then, we conducted a more detailed human evaluation of GNMT and two bespoke models, i.e. the SPOOK and the Novel NMT models. For the automatic evaluation, we used the BLEU (Papineni et al., 2002) and METEOR (Denkowski and Lavie, 2014) metrics, which are based on the correspondence of the MT output and the reference translation. The BLEU score was obtained with the Interactive BLEU score evaluator,[1] which is available on the Tilde platform, whereas the METEOR score was calculated by the automatic machine translation evaluation system METEOR, available on GitHub.[2]

The human evaluation consisted of error analysis of the MT output, an assessment of fluency and adequacy, and a measurement of the temporal dimension of post-editing (PE) effort. Twelve Master's students in translation or interpreting took part in the evaluation. On average, participants had at least four years of translation experience and 83% of them have already had some PE experience. Each translated one excerpt from the novel *Something about you* by Julie James and post-edited the hypotheses of a similar excerpt, while assessing the fluency and adequacy of each segment. The translators were divided into six groups of two: groups A and B evaluated GNMT, C and D evaluated the translations provided by the SPOOK neural model, and E and F by the Novel model. In that way, all three models were evaluated by four participants each and on two excerpts. Participants also provided feedback after the translation via a questionnaire.

Participants translated and post-edited MT outputs using the Post-Editing Tool (PET) interface (Aziz et al., 2012), a CAT tool built for research purposes. PET measures time spent on editing each segment, tracks changes and allows adding optional assessments, which can be configured via a context file. Thus, after confirming a post-edited sentence, participants also assessed its fluency and adequacy on a pop-up assessment page before moving to the next sentence. Prior to the beginning of the assigned tasks, participants were provided with guidelines in order to produce professional quality translations. Moreover, they post-edited automatically generated translation of a short excerpt from the novel *Something about you*,

[1] https://www.letsmt.eu/Bleu.aspx

[2] https://github.com/cmu-mtlab/meteor

containing three sentences, to familiarize themselves with the PET tool and the workflow.

We followed TAUS guidelines for quality evaluation using adequacy and fluency approaches (Berghoefer, 2013). Participants were asked to rate adequacy on a 4-point scale based on the extent to which the meaning, expressed in the source, is also expressed in the MT output. Score 4 means that all meaning is expressed, 3 means most meaning, 2 little meaning and 1 means that no meaning is expressed in the hypothesis provided by the MT system. The second 4-point scale indicates how fluent and grammatically well-formed the hypothetical translation is. In this case, score 4 means that a translation is written in flawless Slovene, 3 means good Slovene, 2 means disfluent Slovene and 1 means that it is incomprehensible. After the assessment, we measured inter-annotation agreement using the kappa coefficient.

In addition to the measuring of the PE effort and assessing fluency and adequacy, we also compared GNMT, the SPOOK and the Novel NMT models based on an error analysis.

4 Results

4.1 Automatic Evaluation

Table 2 shows the results of the automatic evaluation. It revealed that GNMT achieved the best METEOR and BLEU score (30 and 21.97 respectively), followed by Novel with METEOR score of 20.35 and BLEU score of 20.75, and SPOOK with METEOR score of 19.67 and BLEU score of 19.01. These findings refute the first hypothesis predicting that models tailored to literature would achieve better scores than GNMT. On the other hand, the results confirmed the third hypothesis supposing that the Novel model, tailored to a specific author, would perform better than the SPOOK model, trained on a bigger but more varied literary corpus. The lowest score was obtained by the Just Novel model, with two layers. However, a similar model with four layers, trained on the same training set, obtained higher scores, although it produced considerably lower quality translations consisting of just six words. This indicates that BLEU and METEOR scores are not always accurate. The combined SPOOK + Novel model that was trained on the corpus SPOOK and on the corpus, consisting of a novel *Practice Makes Perfect* and its translation, performed worse than the models, trained on just one of those corpora. According to the BLEU metric, it performed even worse than the model, trained solely on out-of-domain data. This contradicts the common belief that the addition of more training data always leads to better results. In the case of the SPOOK + Novel neural model we can also observe a discrepancy between the BLEU and METEOR metrics. According to the METEOR metric, this model outperforms the baseline by 0.62 point, whereas based on the BLEU metric, it achieves 1.48 fewer points. Furthermore, the biggest difference between BLEU and METEOR scores is 8.03 points in the case of GNMT, whereas in the case of another model, the difference is only 0.40 point.

	Baseline	*Just SPOOK (2 layers)*	*Just SPOOK (4 layers)*	*Just Novel (2 layers)*	*Just Novel (4 layers)*	*SPOOK*	*Novel*	*SPOOK + Novel*	*GNMT*
BLEU	17.50	6.61	2.04	1.73	1.78	19.01	20.75	16.02	21.97
METEOR	18.50	11.86	6.98	5.01	5.21	19.67	20.35	19.12	30.00

Table 2. Results of the automatic evaluation

4.2 Measuring Post-Editing Effort

Since the time required for translation and post-editing varied among participants, the models were compared based on the time gains of post-editing. Nevertheless, the evaluation revealed significant discrepancies between post-editors. Table 3 illustrates that the first participant from the group C finished the translation task 7.4 minutes faster than the post-editing task, whereas the second participant from the same group finished the translation task 7.1 minutes slower than the post-editing task. This means that based on the second participant the evaluated model outperforms the other two, whereas based on the first participant, who post-edited the same output, the evaluated model performs the worst. Post-editors already had some experience in PE, they were given guidelines, and they had to post-edit a short excerpt before the evaluation. Therefore, the reason for the discrepancies between post-editors cannot be due to the lack of experience. It is probable that poor results can be attributable to the lack of precision and motivation. It is nonetheless true that no participant had more than 160 hours of PE experience–the equivalent of a month of full-time post-editing–which greatly increases the level of comfort with post-editing (Vasconcellos, 1986). In spite of discrepancies, the findings show that all three NMT approaches resulted in increases in translation productivity. In general, post-editing was revealed to be 1.6% faster than translation from scratch and most participants post-edited a pre-translated excerpt faster than they translated a similar excerpt. Based on the average times of all participants that assessed the same NMT model, the productivity increased the most in the case of GNMT, followed by the Novel and the SPOOK NMT models, as illustrated in Table 4. Most participants perceived post-editing to be faster than translation from scratch, although the perceptions of half of the participants did not match the measurements (highlighted bold in Table 3). Two out of three participants who finished the translation task faster than the PE task wrongly perceived the translation task to be more time-consuming.

Participants perceived the quality of outputs to be overall good or sometimes good. Their answers to the questionnaire revealed that most of them have positive attitudes towards post-editing. They mostly think that MT is more useful in assisting with professional translations of other types of text than literary texts, although some of them believe that might change in the future.

	Group A (person 1)–GNMT	*Group A (person 2)–GNTM*	*Group B (person 1)–GNMT*	*Group B (person 2)–GNMT*	*Group C (person 1)–SPOOK*	*Group C (person 2)–SPOOK*	*Group D (person 1)–SPOOK*	*Group D (person 2)–SPOOK*	*Group E (person 1)–Novel*	*Group E (person 2)–Novel*	*Group F (person 1)–Novel*	*Group F (person 2)–Novel*
Translation time (min)	9.5	12.6	6.0	12.3	17.2	8.4	12.8	14.0	11.7	17.6	10.7	12.1
PE time (min)	12.8	13.0	9.7	16.3	9.8	15.6	13.2	15.9	13.0	21.4	10.6	11.1
Difference between translation and PE time (min)	3.2	0.4	**3.8**	**4.0**	**-7.4**	7.1	**0.4**	1.9	1.3	**3.8**	-0.1	**-1.0**
The task that participants perceived to be more time-consuming	translation	translation	**PE**	**PE**	**transla-tion**	translation	**PE**	translation	translation	**PE**	PE	**transla-tion**

Table 3. Measurement of the temporal dimension of post-editing effort

	GNMT	*SPOOK*	*Novel*
Average difference between translation and PE time (min)	2.9	0.5	1.0

Table 4. Average difference between translation and PE time

4.3 Assessment of Fluency and Adequacy

Based on the assessment of fluency and adequacy, GNMT produced translations of the highest quality, followed by translations provided by the Novel neural model. However, the translations generated by the SPOOK model were given better scores for fluency. The results refute the second hypothesis predicting that models, tailored to literature, would achieve better scores than GNMT. On the other hand, the fourth hypothesis was partially confirmed, since the author-specific model performed better than the model, trained on a mixed literary corpus, according to the temporal dimension of post-editing effort and the assessment of adequacy. However, it obtained lower scores for fluency.

Figure 1 illustrates that not much can be inferred from the participants' assessments of fluency and adequacy. For instance, based on the assessment of the first participant from the group A, we could say that the GNMT produces the most fluent outputs. On the other hand, based on the assessment of the second participant from the same group we could infer that the GNMT's generated translations are the least fluent ones.

Inter-rater agreement on fluency and adequacy proved to be very low. Each hypothesis was evaluated by two participants. In two groups one sentence obtained the highest score in one or both categories by one evaluator and the lowest score by the other. In five out of six groups, one or more sentences were given the second-highest score by one evaluator and the lowest score by the other. In some cases, we can presume that the lowest score was given by mistake, since the evaluator decided that no post-editing is necessary for that segment. In other cases, the low-annotator agreement may be attributable to the issue that there are no clear guidelines on how to assign values to translations.

Inter-rater agreement was also measured using the kappa coefficient. The results revealed mostly slight inter-agreement. In group A, even a negative value occurred in one of the categories, whereas in the other category the inter-annotation agreement of the two participants was moderate, as shown in Figure 2 below.

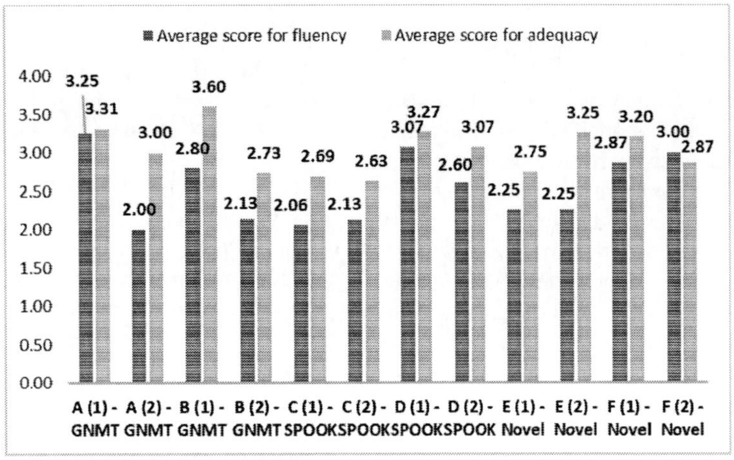

Figure 1. Average score for fluency and adequacy

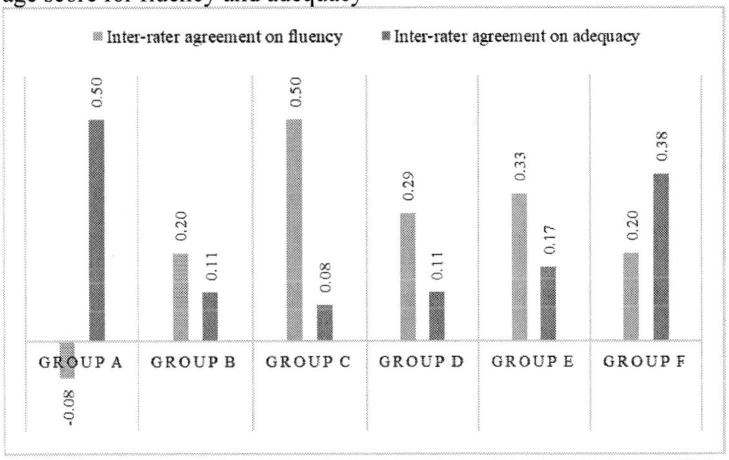

Figure 2. Inter-rater agreement on fluency and adequacy based on the kappa coefficient

4.4 Error Analysis

The error analysis of the translations generated by the GNMT, the Novel and the SPOOK models revealed various punctuation errors, wrong translations of prepositions and conjunctions, inappropriate shifts in verb mood, wrong noun forms and co-reference changes. Regarding semantic errors, the analysis revealed that GNMT assigned the wrong gender to the main character ('Cameron'), the Novel model changed the name of another character, and all three models wrongly translated a proper noun of a hotel ('Peninsula') as a common noun. Many other semantic errors were detected, especially in connection with idioms and ambiguous words. Some expressions, such as "brunch buffet", were inconsistently translated and the analysis revealed that when MT systems encounter a new word, GNMT most often leaves the term untranslated, whereas the SPOOK NMT model is especially prone to inventing words, which do not exist in the Slovene language. In addition to this, all models tend to omit and add words. The analysis revealed that the SPOOK and Novel neural models added or omitted negations, which significantly changes the meaning of the sentence. They also changed numbers, which can be perceived as a serious error in some cases. However, they also changed the American emergency number (911) to the Slovene emergency number (112), which can be perceived as a cultural adaptation. Nevertheless, such attempts can be problematic. For example, the Novel translation model substituted an imperial unit for the metric unit without converting the values, which led to an error.

The outputs of all three NMT models include some unintelligible sentences, as well as some sentences with only punctuation errors. However, there were no sentences that would not need post-editing.

5 Conclusion and Future Work

The automatic and human evaluation revealed that mixed-domain NMT model GNMT, trained on millions of examples, performs better than our models tailored to literature and trained on a much smaller training dataset. However, contrary to popular belief, more data does not always lead to better results, since the Novel NMT model, adapted to a specific author and trained on out-of-domain data and a corpus, consisting of one novel and its translation, outperformed the SPOOK one, trained on out-of-domain data and a bigger corpus, consisting of nine novels, written by various authors. Moreover, the model that was trained on the out-of-domain corpus and on both in-domain corpora performed worse than a model, trained solely on out-of-domain corpus, that is trained on a smaller training dataset. Since the Novel model, adapted to a specific author, came very close to the GNMT translation system based on the BLEU scores, future studies could fruitfully explore this issue further by training the model with more novels written by the same author. In our case, there are seven other novels by Julie James translated to Slovene that could be added to the training dataset.

In general, post-editing was revealed to be 1.6% faster than translation from scratch and most participants post-edited an excerpt faster than they translated a similar excerpt, which are promising results for literary machine translation from English to Slovene.

Moreover, the findings suggest that the assessment of fluency and adequacy and measurement of the temporal dimension of post-editing effort might not be reliable as evaluation methods. This assumption could be addressed in future studies which could be conducted on a larger scale, with more participants, preferably more experienced in post-editing, who would perform the task in a professional setting.

6 Acknowledgements

This publication has emanated from research supported in part by a research grant from Science Foundation Ireland (SFI) under Grant Number SFI/12/RC/2289 (Insight), co-funded by the European Regional Development Fund.

References

Arčan, Mihael. 2018. A Comparison of Statistical and Neural Machine Translation for Slovene, Serbian and Croatian. *Proceedings of the Conference on Language Technologies and Digital Humanities*, Ljubljana, Slovenia. 3–10.

Arčan, Mihael, Maja Popović, and Paul Buitelaar. 2016. Asistent – A Machine Translation System for Slovene, Serbian and Croatian. *Proceedings of the Conference on Language Technologies and Digital Humanities*, Ljubljana, Slovenia. 13–20.

Aziz, Wilker, Sheila Castilho M. de Sousa, and Lucia Specia. 2012. PET: a tool for post-editing and assessing machine translation. *The Eighth International Conference on Language Resources and Evaluation, LREC'12*, Istanbul, Turkey. 3982–3987.

Berghoefer, Karin. 2013. *TAUS Best Practice Guidelines Quality Evaluation using Adequacy and/or Fluency Approaches*. URL: https://www.taus.net/index.php?option=com_rsfiles&layout=preview&tmpl=component&path=Articles%2Ftaus-adequacy-fluencyguidelines-may2013.pdf.

Besacier, Laurent. 2014. Traduction automatisée d'une oeuvre littéraire: une étude pilote. *Traitement Automatique du Langage Naturel (TALN)*, Marseille, France. 389–394.

Callison-Burch, Chris, Cameron Fordyce, Philipp Koehn, Christof Monz, and Josh Schroeder. 2007. (meta-) evaluation of machine translation. *Proceedings of the Second Workshop on Statistical Machine Translation*. 136–158.

Denkowski, Michael, and Alon Lavie. 2014. Meteor universal: Language specific translation evaluation for any target language. *Proceedings of the EACL 2014 Workshop on Statistical Machine Translation*.

Donaj, Gregor, and Mirjam Sepesy Maučec. 2018. Prehod iz statističnega strojnega prevajanja na prevajanje z nevronskimi omrežji za jezikovni par slovenščina-angleščina. *Zbornik konference Jezikovne tehnologije in digitalna humanistika*, 62–68. Ljubljana University Press, Faculty of Arts, Ljubljana, Slovenia.

Etchegoyhen, Thierry, Lindsay Bywood, Mark Fishel, Panayota Georgakopoulou, Jie Jiang, Gerard Van Loenhout, Arantza Del Pozo, Mirjam Sepesy Maučec, Anja Turner, and Martin Volk. 2014. Machine Translation for Subtitling: A Large-Scale Evaluation. *Proceedings of the Ninth International Conference on Language Resources and Evaluation (LREC14)*, Reykjavik, Iceland. 46–53.

Genzel, Dmitriy, Jakob Uszkoreit, and Franz Och. 2010. "Poetic" Statistical Machine Translation: Rhyme and Meter. *Proceedings of the 2010 Conference on Empirical Methods in Natural Language Processing, EMNLP '10*. 158–166.

Gouws, Stephan, and Mostafa Dehghani. 2018. Moving Beyond Translation with the Universal Transformer. *Google AI Blog*, Google, 15 August 2018, https://ai.googleblog.com/2018/08/moving-beyond-translation-with.html.

Greene, Erica, Tugba Bodrumlu, and Kevin Knight. 2010. Automatic analysis of rhythmic poetry with applications to generation and translation. *Proceedings of the 2010 conference on empirical methods in natural language processing.* 524–533.

Hari, Daniel. 2018. *Pregled prosto dostopnih strojnih prevajalnikov*. Thesis, University of Maribor.

Jones, Ruth, and Ann Irvine. 2013. The (un)faithful machine translator. *Proceedings of the 7th Workshop on Language Technology for Cultural Heritage, Social Sciences, and Humanities.* 96–101.

Klein, Guillaume, Yoon Kim, Yuntian Deng, Jean Senellart, and Alexander M. Rush. 2017. Opennmt: Opensource toolkit for neural machine translation.

Krek, Simon. 2012. *Slovenski jezik v digitalni dobi – The Slovene Language in the Digital Age*. META-NET White Paper Series. Springer.

Landis, J. Richard, and Gary G. Koch. 1977. The measurement of observer agreement for categorical data. B*iometrics*, 33:159–174.

Le, Quoc V., and Mike Schuster. 2016. A Neural Network for Machine Translation, at Production Scale. *Google AI Blog*, Google, 27 September 2016, https://ai.googleblog.com/2016/09/a-neural-network-for-machine.html.

Moorkens, Joss, Antonio Toral, Sheila Castilho, and Andy Way. 2018. Translators' perceptions of literary post-editing using statistical and neural machine translation. *Translation Spaces* 7(2): 240–262.

Papineni, Kishore, Salim Roukos, Todd Ward, and Wei-Jing Zhu. 2002. BLEU: a method for automatic evaluation of machine translation. *Proceedings of the 40th Annual Meeting on Association for Computational Linguistics, ACL '02*. 311–318.

Romih, Miro, and Peter Holozan. 2002. Slovensko-angleški prevajalni sistem (a Slovene-English translation system). *Proceedings of the 3rd Language Technologies Conference*, Ljubljana, Slovenia.

Schuster, Mike, Melvin Johnson, and Nikhil Thorat. 2016. Zero-Shot Translation with Google's Multilingual Neural Machine Translation System. *Google AI Blog*, Google, 22 November 2016, https://ai.googleblog.com/2016/11/zero-shot-translation-with-googles.html.

Tiedemann, Jörg. 2012. Character-based pivot translations for under-resourced languages and domains. *Proceedings of the 13th Conference of the European Chapter of the Association for Computational Linguistics (EACL)*, Avignon, France. 141–151.

Toral, Antonio, and Andy Way. 2018. What Level of Quality Can Neural Machine Translation Attain on Literary Text?: From Principles to Practice. *Translation Quality Assessment*, 263–287. Springer, Cham, Switzerland.

Toral, Antonio, and Andy Way. 2015. Translating Literary Text between Related Languages using SMT. *Proceedings of the Fourth Workshop on Computational Linguistics for Literature*, Denver, Colorado, USA. 123–132.

Uszkoreit, Jakob. 2017. Transformer: A Novel Neural Network Architecture for Language Understanding. *Google AI Blog*, Google 31 August 2017, https://ai.googleblog.com/2017/08/transformer-novel-neural-network.html.

Vasconcellos, Muriel. 1986. Post-editing On-screen: Machine Translation from Spanish into English. *Proceedings of Translating and the Computer* 8, London, UK. 133–146.

Vintar, Špela. 2018. Terminology Translation Accuracy in Statistical versus Neural MT: An Evaluation for the English-Slovene Language Pair. *Proceedings of the Eleventh International Conference on Language Resources and Evaluation (LREC 2018)*, Miyazaki, Japan.

Vintar, Špela. 2013. Uvodnik: o rojstvu korpusa SPOOK in njegovih prvih sadovih. *Slovenski prevodi skozi korpusno prizmo*, 6–13. Ljubljana University Press, Faculty of Arts, Ljubljana, Slovenia.

The Challenges of Using Neural Machine Translation for Literature

Evgeny Matusov
AppTek
Aachen, Germany
ematusov@apptek.com

Abstract

In this paper, we adapt state-of-the-art neural machine translation (NMT) systems to literary content and use them to translate fiction stories from English to Russian and from German to English. We show that such adapted systems have richer vocabulary and lead to improved automatic evaluation metrics on literary prose as compared to general domain NMT systems, including Google's online MT. We propose a new error classification scheme for NMT output that is specifically tailored to literary translation and let a bilingual evaluator analyze translated excerpts from two fiction stories. The results show that up to 30% of machine-translated sentences have acceptable quality. We observe very few severe syntactic errors even on complex sentences, but the meaning errors for ambiguous words are still numerous. A separate classification of consistency, pronoun resolution, and tone/register error types reveals a high potential of MT quality improvement by considering the context of previous sentences or even the whole story. A preliminary experiment aimed at reducing pronoun translation errors confirms this potential.

1 Introduction

Recent advances in neural machine translation led to a greater acceptance of MT technology, even among professional translators. However, it is hard to find anyone who would dare to use NMT for the professional translation of literature. Yet we believe that the challenges of literature translation could be tackled with NMT.

In this work, we adapted a baseline general domain NMT system, described in Section 3, to the style and diverse vocabulary of literary translations. The details of the adaptation process are given in Section 4. This was carried out on two language pairs: English-to-Russian and German-to-English. We then computed automatic error measures for translations of entire short novels and were able to show improvements as compared to the baseline model and Google's online MT (Section 5).

Next, we performed a thorough manual evaluation of both human and automatic translation quality on an excerpt from each novel. For better insights into the shortcomings of NMT and potential improvements, we devised a novel error classification scheme, as described in Section 6.2, intended to tackle errors characteristic of neural MT systems, including cohesion and inter-sentence context issues which are prominent in literary translation. Sections 6.3 and 6.4 describe these experiments in detail and also provide a quantitative comparison between Google's online and AppTek's adapted NMT for each error type.

We conclude the paper with a discussion on the possible applications of NMT for literature and underline the challenges, but also the opportunities associated with state-of-the-art NMT technology and its future developments.

2 Related Work

Using MT for literary translation has been inconceivable not only to professional translators of prose, but also to most MT researchers. As the technology made significant progress in the last decade, initial research in this direction appeared, although non-computational linguists remain largely skeptical (Almahasees and Mustafa, 2017). Voigt and Jurafsky (2012) identified that incorporating discourse features above the sentence level is an important requirement for literary translation because of the greater referential cohesion of literary texts, but did not run any MT experiments with systems adapted to such content. In a pilot study, Besacier and Schwartz (2015) trained a phrase-based statistical MT system for translating a short story from English to French, concluding that a faster literary translation with post-editing can be achieved at the expense of translator creativity and freedom of expression. Toral and Way (2018) compared phrase-based statistical MT with neural MT when translating literary content using automatic and human evaluation. They concluded that neural MT significantly outperforms phrase-based SMT in this genre, but "fills the gap" to the human quality level only by 20%. In that work, a vanilla NMT architecture for English-to-Catalan MT was used, not described in detail. The authors built a relatively large in-domain parallel corpus of human-translated fiction, and also use synthetic parallel data, for which Catalan novels are translated using a phrase-based system into English. In contrast, in our work we use the latest and best NMT architecture both for back-translation of large volumes of novels, and for the actual MT experiments; with only a very small parallel fiction corpus we are still able to obtain improvements over a strong general-domain NMT baseline.

Other related work important to literary translation include style transfer (Korotkova et al., 2018) and personalization (Rabinovich et al., 2016), number and gender disambiguation (Moryossef et al., 2019), document-level translation (Wang et al., 2017).

This work focuses on translation of prose; however, there have also been attempts to automatically translate poetry, with rhyming and rhythmical constraints, starting from the seminal work of Genzel et al. (2010) for phrase-based SMT. Recently, neural architectures were also proposed for this task (Ghazvininejad et al., 2018).

3 AppTek's Neural Machine Translation System

AppTek's NMT system is based on the the RETURNN toolkit (Zeyer et al., 2018) that implements training and inference in TensorFlow (Abadi et al., 2015). We trained two different architectures of NMT models: an attention-based RNN model similar to (Bahdanau et al., 2015) with additive attention for English-to-Russian and a Transformer model (Vaswani et al., 2017) with multi-head attention for German-to-English.

In the RNN-based attention model, both the source and the target words are projected into a 620-dimensional embedding space. The models are equipped with 4 layers of bidirectional encoder using LSTM cells with 1000 units. A unidirectional decoder with the same number of units was used in all cases. We applied a layer-wise pretraining scheme that lead to both better convergence and faster training speed during the initial pre-train epochs (Zeyer et al., 2018).

In the Transformer model, both the self-attentive encoder and the decoder consist of 6 stacked layers. Every layer is composed of two sub-layers: an 8-head self-attention layer followed by a rectified linear unit (ReLU). We applied layer normalization (Ba et al., 2016) before each sub-layer, whereas dropout (Srivastava et al., 2014) and residual connection (He et al., 2016) were applied afterwards. Our model is very similar to "base" Transformer of the original paper (Vaswani et al., 2017), such that all projection layers and the multi-head attention layers consist of 512 nodes followed by a feed-forward layer equipped with 2048 nodes.

We trained all models using the Adam optimizer (Kingma and Ba, 2015) with a learning rate of 0.001 for the attention RNN-based model and 0.0003 for the Transformer model. We applied a learning rate scheduling similar to the Newbob scheme based on the perplexity on the validation set for several consecutive evaluation checkpoints. We also employed label smoothing of 0.1 (Pereyra et al., 2017) for all trainings. The dropout rate ranged from 0.1 to 0.3.

AppTek's general domain English-to-Russian system was trained for roughly 3 epochs on 25 million sentence pairs (265M words on the English side). The corresponding German-to-English system was trained on 47M sentence pairs (752M running words on the English side) for less than 2 epochs.

4 Adaptation to Literary Content

First, AppTek's NMT had to be adapted to the style and diverse vocabulary of literary translations. In our experiments, we selected 2.3M sentences (23.5M running words) from books in Russian[1] and translated them using AppTek's general domain Russian-to-English NMT system. Following the approach of (Sennrich et al., 2016a), we then used the resulting parallel corpus as synthetic data, mixing it with the data that was used to train AppTek's general domain system from English to Russian. As parallel in-domain data, we used a small corpus of sentence-aligned texts[2] and the OPUS Books collection corpus[3] (Tiedemann, 2012), with a total of 270K sentence pairs and 5.2M running words on the English side.

We followed the same back-translation procedure for German-to-English, randomly selecting 10M sentences (155M running words) from English literature that we downloaded from the Gutenberg[4] project. Again, AppTek's highly competitive English-to-German general-domain Transformer model (Matusov et al., 2018) was used to translate these sentences, so that a synthetic parallel corpus could be used together with the other parallel data in NMT training of the reverse translation direction that was of interest to us. The in-domain parallel data consisted only of the small OPUS Books corpus with less than 50K sentence pairs and ca. 1.2M words on the English side.

We trained the system until convergence in terms of BLEU scores on held-out tuning data. For English-to-Russian, these were contiguous passages of Tolstoy's *Anna Karenina* (here, the input was the English translation, and Tolstoy's writing was used as the reference) and Chesterton's *The Innocence of Father Brown*. For English-to-German, the tuning set was the complete text of Kafka's *Der Prozess* from the OPUS Books collection.

5 Experimental Results

In this section, we review the automatic scores for the generated literature translations. We compute case-insensitive BLEU and TER scores (Papineni et al., 2002; Snover et al., 2006).

[1]The books are publicly available from lib.ru and other sources.
[2]Crawled from http://multitran.ru.
[3]http://opus.nlpl.eu/Books.php
[4]https://www.gutenberg.org

System	BLEU [%]	TER [%]
Google	13.9	84.6
AppTek	14.2	83.7
+ adaptation	15.2	82.5

Table 1: Automatic MT quality measurements for English-to-Russian literary translation.

System	BLEU [%]	TER [%]
Google	20.2	67.2
AppTek	18.5	69.7
+ adaptation	16.2	71.0

Table 2: Automatic MT quality measurements for German-to-English literary translation.

5.1 English-to-Russian

We evaluated the quality of Google's online MT, AppTek's general domain and literature-adapted NMT on four sentence-aligned stories by Conan-Doyle (*The Lift*, *Scandal in the Bohemia*) Poe, (*The Pit and the Pendelum*), and Chesterton (*The Invisible Man*). Thus, the test set was comprised of 1646 sentences and 30K words on the English side.

The experimental results are summarized in Table 1. First, we see that the BLEU scores are much lower than those of state-of-the-art systems on newswire and news commentary texts as evaluated e.g. at WMT 2019[5] (the BLEU scores there are mostly over 30%). This supports the assumption about the particular difficulty of literary translation, but, as we will discuss in Section 6.1, also highlights serious errors in human reference translation.

Google's online NMT and AppTek's baseline system both perform at similar level, with AppTek's system showing marginally better scores on literary content. AppTek's En-Ru system adapted to literary content improves over the general domain baseline by 1% BLEU absolute and thus also outperforms Google's online MT (15.2 vs. 13.9% BLEU). However, as we will see in Section 6.3, these score improvements do not necessarily mean better translation quality according to human analysis.

5.2 German-to-English

For German-to-English, the test set we chose was Franz Kafka's *Verwandlung* with 675 sentences and ca. 20K German words; interestingly, this cor-

[5]http://matrix.statmt.org/matrix/systems_list/1914

pus was also selected by (Cap et al., 2015) for their experiments on co-reference resolution in literary texts, where they argue that a co-reference resolution algorithm can be improved by features derived from word alignment to a human translation of the text into another language.

Table 2 summarizes the automatic error measures for Google's online MT, Apptek's general domain and adapted NMT. Google's system outperforms Apptek's systems for this language pair, but as the human analysis will show in Section 6.4, there were error categories, for which AppTek's output had less errors. The adaptation using back-translated English literature did not result in BLEU and TER score improvements, but again a bilingual evaluator confirmed that the output of the adapted system was better across multiple error categories. This underlines again that automatic MT error measures are not reliable for judging the quality of literary translation.

6 Error Analysis

We employed a bilingual evaluator fluent in the source and target languages to perform an error analysis of the MT output on parts of the test set, i.e. on the excerpts of Conan-Doyle and Kafka stories for English-to-Russian and German-to-English, respectively.

6.1 Human Translation Quality

Before dealing with MT output, the human expert thoroughly checked the human reference translations by comparing them to the source sentences.

To our surprise, the Russian human translation had a significant number of errors. Some of them (5 in total) could be explained by wrong automatic sentence alignment, where a part of the reference translation for a given segment actually was a translation of (a part of) the previous or the next segment. However, we also noticed other unexpected errors, including simplifications, omissions, and meaning change, which, in our opinion, go beyond the usual freedom of a translator to deviate from literal translation of the original text. Here are some examples:

- *Don't worry, my darling, the cloud will roll off.* is translated into Не волнуйся, дорогая, всё пройдёт [*don't worry, dear, all will pass*] which means that the translator could not find a good idiomatic equivalent and translated the idiom as "everything will pass".
- *Then it lifts quite suddenly, like a mist in the sunshine.* For this sentence, the translator completely reversed the meaning of the verb "lifts", translating it into появляется, "appears".
- The word *nightmare* is translated into ночной кошмар [*night nightmare*], an error that a professional translator can't afford to make.
- The term *side show* is omitted from the translation, perhaps because it was hard for the translator in Russia in the pre-Internet era to check what it means.
- *It's hung up, but the gear is being overhauled.* The sentence was translated as Немного задерживаемся, механизм осматривают. [*(We are) somewhat delayed, mechanism is being looked at.*] Here, the first part of the sentence is translated as "we are a bit delayed", although it is clear from the context that the gear is stuck, which has more consequences than a simple delay.
- *... a man who was descending the steel framework.* The phrase was translated as ... человек, который опускал вниз стальной каркас. [*... man, who brought down the steel carcass.*] Here, the translator thought that the man brought down the steel framework, although it is clear from previous and subsequent sentences that the man was climbing down the framework of the lift shaft.

Overall, there were 29 errors in 111 segments which significantly altered the meaning intended by the author and/or omitted translations of some words or phrases.

For Kafka's translation into English, the situation is somewhat better: here, we found only 7 errors, and only two segmentation errors. An example of a severe error is a translation of the sentence *Gregor war während seines fünfjährigen Dienstes noch nicht einmal krank gewesen*, which was translated into "in fifteen years of service Gregor had never once yet been ill", whereas actually Gregor was only employed for 5 years. Another error where the meaning is completely reversed was noted in the translation of the following segment: *Gregor erschrak, als er seine antwortende Stimme hörte, die wohl unverkennbar seine frühere war...* This was translated into "Gregor was shocked when he heard his own voice answering, it could hardly be recognised as the voice he had had before...".

6.2 MT Error Classification

In previous work, a number or MT error classification schemes have been proposed (Flanagan, 1994; Popović and Ney, 2011; Costa et al., 2015). All of them were either linguistically motivated or designed with the goal of identifying and classifying errors (semi-)automatically. After analyzing literature translation output, we have come to a different classification that specifically addresses higher-quality neural machine translation and highlights errors which can be fixed with additional context or information. We also introduce an idiom translation error category which is very important for literature.

Here are the proposed categories in detail:

1. *M1: severe meaning error.* A word or a short phrase is translated into a word or phrase in the target language with a wrong meaning given the context, and this translation is misleading to the reader. The reader can not easily recover the original meaning without seeing the source sentence. For NMT systems, in most cases these are ambiguous words or phrases, since wrong translations into something completely unrelated are rare, except for unknown/rare words, for which we introduce a separate category below.

2. *M2: minor meaning error.* A translated word or a short phrase conveys the original meaning that was intended in the source language, but with slight deviations. Usually, a synonym is used that has a slightly different meaning or is stylistically or otherwise not appropriate given the context. Yet the intent of the author can be understood from the translation and a better formulation can be guessed by the reader without consulting the source sentence.

3. *U: unknown word or segmentation error.* The vast majority of NMT systems use subwords (Sennrich et al., 2016b; Kudo and Richardson, 2018) to represent translation units. Thus, any out-of-vocabulary (OOV) word is separated into several known subwords. This does not guarantee a correct translation of the OOV word in any way. Moreover, known rare words may be translated incorrectly if the subwords of such a word have a pronounced different meaning. We group all such errors in a single category; in most cases these errors are directly visible in the MT output (e.g. wrong transliteration, translation of only a part of a word, etc.). For source languages without explicit word segmentation, such as Chinese, this category would also contain MT errors resulting from incorrect word segmentation.

4. *C: Consistency/term translation error.* This category specifically addresses translation consistency for words and phrases that, in the context of a particular document, should have a unique translation (apart from morphological variation) throughout the document. Examples include names and name transliterations, as well as technical or other terms (cf. *Flying Service* in Conan-Doyle's text and *Prokurist* in Kafka's text).

5. *P: pronoun resolution error.* As the MT quality improved with neural systems, these errors, which in many cases can be avoided only by consulting the context of the previous sentence(s) or even the whole document have become more visible, hence we introduced a separate category for them.

6. *L: locution error.* Whereas such errors could be categorized as meaning errors, we introduce a separate category for wrong locution or idiom translation. An idiom translation is considered wrong if the idiom is translated word-for-word, which significantly distorts its meaning in the target language, or into an idiom that has a different meaning or a similar meaning, but is incomplete/erroneously formulated.

7. *O, I, R: omission, insertion, repetition errors.* These three error categories have been frequently used in the MT community. Whereas, as our analysis shows, insertion errors (insertion of an unrelated word or phrase) are very rare in NMT output, omissions, i.e. untranslated word sequences, still happen, especially in longer sentences. Repetition errors include not only repetitions of single words or phrases, but repetitions with conjunctions (e.g. "red and red") or repetitions in a differ-

ent word form "wooden wood" or constructs such as "doorbell door".

8. *S1: severe syntax error.* The structure of the translated sentence is not correct. It can't be parsed by a human, or the incorrect syntax distorts the meaning of the entire sentence, even though the meaning of individual words and short phrases is conveyed correctly. Examples include passive constructions with subject/object wrongly swapped, wrong tense, wrong attachment of prepositional phrases, morphological disagreement leading to parsing ambiguity, etc. To some extent, there is overlap with M1, but the S1 errors can not be easily localized to a single word/phrase.

9. *S2: minor syntax error.* The translated sentence contains minor syntactic or morphological errors, which can be easily corrected without significant changes to the sentence. Examples may include wrong verb tense without meaning distortion (e.g. simple vs. progressive), morphological agreement between noun and adjective, a not very appropriate preposition where a better one can be easily guessed, etc.

10. *T: tone/register error.* These errors may affect multiple words in a sentence, but only one error per sentence is counted. Examples include a wrong "you"-form and corresponding verb forms (polite vs. informal), word forms addressing a male when from previous context it is clear that a female should be addressed, etc. Another example is a formally correct translation of German "man kann" into English as "one can" or "you can", which is in practice often not appropriate. Also, the usage of stylistically inappropriate words and phrases (e.g. colloquialisms) falls under this category.

6.3 English-to-Russian MT

Table 3 summarizes the results of the error analysis performed by a bilingual evaluator according to the error classification described in Section 6.2. The error analysis was performed separately for each of the systems analyzed (Google's online MT and AppTek's NMT adapted to literary content) on the first 114 segments of A. Conan-Doyle's *The Lift*, which was part of the test set mentioned in Section 5.1. In Table 3, we also show the BLEU and TER scores on these segments only. The human expert had access to all 114 segments at once when marking/counting errors in the MT output. The 114 segments contained 1489 English words.

We observed that although BLEU and TER improvements of the AppTek's adapted system are substantial, they are not reflected in human analysis. Approximately 20% of segments for both MT systems did not contain any errors (OK) and thus would not require any further processing by a professional translator or post-editor. AppTek's MT output has fewer severe meaning errors (30 vs. 33) and fewer minor syntax errors (22 vs. 29). However, this comes at the expense of an increased number of minor meaning errors, where a wrong synonym is used (30 vs. 20). One can argue, however, that these errors by definition can be fixed by a monolingual post-editor of the target language.

Given the small sample size of 114 sentences, the number of consistency (C) and pronoun resolution (P), and tone/register errors (T) is rather high and suggests that document-level context is necessary to improve performance. For consistency errors, terminology override could be used to enforce e.g. that "the lift" is translated always as подъемник and not лифт, but it is an open research problem how to achieve this in morphologically rich target languages, where multiple word forms of the desired term translation may have to be produced (in this example, up to six different noun cases of подъемник).

The number of omission errors (O) is high (7 and 11), which supports previous findings about NMT errors. On the other hand, the number of serious syntax errors is low, which again supports the argument that NMT systems generally produce fluent and syntactically correct output. This also suggests that the post-editing required to fix the remaining errors would probably be local in most cases, where only single words or groups of words would have to be corrected, as opposed to re-structuring the entire sentence. A good example for such minimal post-editing is the following MT output for a complex sentence from one of the systems: Барнс, рабочий, пробормотал, что что-то должно быть не так, и прыгнул, как кошка, через щель, отделявшую их от решетки из металла, он вылез из поля зрения. The English sentence was: *Barnes, the workman, mut-*

System	BLEU	TER	OK	M1	M2	U	C	P	L	O	R	I	S1	S2	T	Total
Google	11.1	86.4	22	33	20	2	13	6	9	7	3	0	2	29	5	129
AppTek	13.6	80.8	23	30	30	2	12	10	11	11	4	0	4	22	10	146

Table 3: Human error analysis and BLEU and TER scores in % on the first 114 segments of A. Conan-Doyle's *The Lift* of Google's online MT and AppTek's literature-adapted NMT. The acronyms of the error categories are explained in Section 6.2.

tered that something must be amiss, and springing like a cat across the gap which separated them from the trellis-work of metal he clambered out of sight. Here, it is enough to fix one letter, changing the past tense verb прыгнул [*jumped*] into a gerund прыгнув [*jumping, springing*].

Finally, the high number of idiom translation errors (L) indicates a high number of idioms in the text by Conan-Doyle (mostly spoken by the characters of *The Lift*), and the inability of NMT systems to translate them. Here, idiom dictionaries could be of help, but unfortunately, they are rarely available in electronic form and are in most cases not used by MT system developers because of copyright issues.

6.4 German-to-English MT

Table 4 summarizes the results of the analysis by the bilingual human expert of the MT output for the first 114 segments of F. Kafka's *Die Verwandlung*. The 114 segments contained 2478 German words, which means that the sentence length here is on average 66% longer than for the English-to-Russian segments analyzed in the previous section. Nevertheless, the total number of errors is slightly lower for En-De than for En-Ru, which shows a higher level of MT quality for this language pair. Overall, 28-30% of the segments were considered as acceptable by the bilingual evaluator, which is also higher than for English-to-Russian.

Again, although the BLEU scores on these segments show that the Google online system is significantly better, the error analysis reflects this only in part. For instance, AppTek's output has no repetition or insertion errors, and fewer omission and severe syntax errors than Google's output. On the other hand, Google is somewhat better at meaning preservation (M1 and M2 errors).

The high quality of translations from German to English can be illustrated with multiple examples using sentences with complex structure, see Table 5. From the examples of AppTek's literature-adapted NMT, we can see that a richer vocabulary is used (e.g. the words "recollected", "alas", "enveloped", "clumsy"). In fact, we measured a 4% larger vocabulary in the AppTek's translation of *Die Verwandlung* as compared to Google's output.

To test whether pronoun resolution errors can be avoided by introducing the context of the previous source sentence, we trained a variant of the adapted model in which we joined two subsequent short German sentences from the same document with a special separator symbol, whenever the second sentence contained a pronoun and the total number of words in the joined sentence did not exceed 50. The joining was done also for the corresponding English sentences to make valid training sentence pairs. Such data was then added to the original training data. At translation time, we did the joining on the source side only, and then evaluated only the part of the MT output after the generated separator symbol. The result did not change the BLEU score significantly (it increased from 18.2 to 18.7), but two pronoun errors were corrected[6] for the following Kafka's text: *Sollte der Wecker nicht geläutet haben? [Should not the alarm-clock have been ringing?] Man sah vom Bett aus, daß er auf vier Uhr richtig eingestellt war; gewiß hatte er auch geläutet.* Here, if the second sentence is translated separately by the AppTek's literature-adapted system, the translation is "It was seen from the bed that he was properly set at four o'clock; certainly he had also ringed." Google's translation also makes similar pronoun translation errors: "From the bed you could see that he was right at four o'clock; he had certainly rung, too.". In contrast, our system that was additionally trained on joined pairs of sentences and also encoded the previous sentence, produced a much better output: "It was seen from the bed that it was set to four o'clock; surely it was ringing."

The preliminary experiment above showed that it is possible to benefit from inter-sentence context for literature translation. It remains to be seen what NMT architecture and, more importantly, evaluation criteria are most suitable for this endeavour.

[6]The training of the system in question finished too late for a full human analysis, so here we only looked at the sentences with previously identified pronoun resolution errors.

System	BLEU	TER	OK	M1	M2	U	C	P	L	O	R	I	S1	S2	T	Total
Google	22.9	64.0	36	25	22	2	11	9	4	17	3	1	6	23	2	125
AppTek	18.2	67.7	32	31	24	6	9	9	3	14	0	0	4	30	2	132

Table 4: Human error analysis and BLEU and TER scores in % on the first 114 segments of F. Kafka's *Die Verwandlung* of Google's online MT and AppTek's literature-adapted NMT. The acronyms of the error categories are explained in Section 6.2.

German source (F. Kafka)	Human Reference	Google's online MT	AppTek's adapted NMT
Er lag auf seinem panzerartig harten Rücken und sah, wenn er den Kopf ein wenig hob, seinen gewölbten, braunen, von bogenförmigen Versteifungen geteilten Bauch, auf dessen Höhe sich die Bettdecke, zum gänzlichen Niedergleiten bereit, kaum noch erhalten konnte.	He lay on his armour-like back, and if he lifted his head a little he could see his brown belly, slightly domed and divided by arches into stiff sections. The bedding was hardly able to cover it and seemed ready to slide off any moment.	He lay on his panzerartig hard back and saw, if he raised his head a little, his arched, brown, divided by arc-shaped stiffened stomach on the height of the blanket, ready for total descent, could barely maintain.	He lay on his armor-like hard back, and saw, when he lifted his head a little, his vaulted, brown belly, divided by bow-shaped stiffenings, on the height of which the duvet, ready for complete slipping, could scarcely yet be preserved.
In solchen Augenblicken richtete er die Augen möglichst scharf auf das Fenster, aber leider war aus dem Anblick des Morgennebels, der sogar die andere Seite der engen Straße verhüllte, wenig Zuversicht und Munterkeit zu holen.	At times like this he would direct his eyes to the window and look out as clearly as he could, but unfortunately, even the other side of the narrow street was enveloped in morning fog and the view had little confidence or cheer to offer him.	At such moments he aimed his eyes as sharply as possible at the window, but unfortunately, the sight of the morning mist, which even covered the other side of the narrow street, did not bring much confidence and cheerfulness.	At such moments he directed his eyes as sharply _ to the window, but, alas, from the sight of the morning mist, which even enveloped the other side of the narrow street, was to fetch little confidence and murmur.
Er erinnerte sich, schon öfters im Bett irgendeinen vielleicht durch ungeschicktes Liegen erzeugten, leichten Schmerz empfunden zu haben, der sich dann beim Aufstehen als reine Einbildung herausstellte, und er war gespannt, wie sich seine heutigen Vorstellungen allmählich auflösen würden.	He remembered that he had often felt a slight pain in bed, perhaps caused by lying awkwardly, but that had always turned out to be pure imagination and he wondered how his imaginings would slowly resolve themselves today.	He remembered having often felt in bed some slight pain, perhaps awkward, that turned out to be pure imagination when he got up, and he wondered how his present ideas would gradually dissolve.	He recollected having often felt some slight pain caused by clumsy lying in the bed, which then turned out to be pure imagination when getting up, and he was eager to see how his present notions would gradually dissolve.

Table 5: Examples of German-to-English NMT quality. Substantial MT errors are highlighted in red, good word and phrase choices in green.

7 Conclusions and Discussion

In this work, we challenged the assumption that MT is not suitable for literary translation. We adapted state-of-the-art neural MT systems for English-to-Russian and German-to-English to Russian and English fiction, respectively, by using back-translated data and observed that such adaptation leads to improved translation quality according to automatic evaluation metrics. We then asked a bilingual evaluator to thoroughly analyze the adapted MT output according to a novel error taxonomy tailored specifically to NMT errors and potential areas for improvement, with the following observations:

- Up to 30% of evaluated segments, mostly short sentences, were considered acceptable and might only require proof-reading by a monolingual editor of the target language.
- NMT of German fiction into English subjectively has higher quality than NMT of English literature into Russian; in fact the quality is often high enough to understand and even enjoy the story.
- Longer sentences are translated well in terms of syntactic structure, so that the necessary post-editing is often local and minor.
- Automatic evaluation using a single, often badly sentence-aligned human reference is unreliable; moreover, the human translation may contain severe meaning and other (e.g. omission) errors.
- There is significant potential to improve MT quality beyond genre adaptation by using inter-sentence context. This is especially true for consistent translation of character names,

places, as well as pronoun resolution and translation style (e.g. formal vs. non-formal).

To conclude, we would like to elaborate on potential use cases of NMT for literature. Automatic translation of literature may be useful not only for helping professional literature translators in a post-editing scenario. It can also help to make largely undiscovered foreign language books instantly available online to readers worldwide, e.g. when they are translated into English. Publishers could also use NMT to better familiarize themselves with such foreign literary works and be aided in their selection process of books to professionally translate into another language, thus promoting an increased circulation of high-quality work among different languages and cultures.

Automatic translation of prose in combination with MT quality estimation methods could also be used to identify segments which are difficult to translate, or where there is a higher likelihood for a translator to make an error. Literary translations are rarely proof-read by bilinguals, but rather a monolingual editor of the target language edits the translation before publication, a process during which there is a risk of errors being introduced in the text. We argue that a higher level of quality control of literary translation is necessary, and NMT systems could prove to be useful tools to facilitate and speed up this process.

In another application, a good book translated by NMT with consistent name translations could facilitate its crowd-sourced translation (similarly to crowd-sourced subtitling for popular films and series), which could lead to improved quality of such fan translations. Finally, automatic translation may assist foreign language learners with specific phrases they have trouble understanding when reading a book in said foreign language, and thus NMT could have useful applications in foreign language learning as well.

Acknowledgements

The author would like to thank Yota Georgakopoulou for helpful feedback on the first version of this paper.

References

Abadi, Martín, Ashish Agarwal, Paul Barham, Eugene Brevdo, Zhifeng Chen, Craig Citro, Greg S. Corrado, Andy Davis, Jeffrey Dean, Matthieu Devin, Sanjay Ghemawat, Ian Goodfellow, Andrew Harp, Geoffrey Irving, Michael Isard, Yangqing Jia, Rafal Jozefowicz, Lukasz Kaiser, Manjunath Kudlur, Josh Levenberg, Dandelion Mané, Rajat Monga, Sherry Moore, Derek Murray, Chris Olah, Mike Schuster, Jonathon Shlens, Benoit Steiner, Ilya Sutskever, Kunal Talwar, Paul Tucker, Vincent Vanhoucke, Vijay Vasudevan, Fernanda Viégas, Oriol Vinyals, Pete Warden, Martin Wattenberg, Martin Wicke, Yuan Yu, and Xiaoqiang Zheng. 2015. TensorFlow: Large-scale machine learning on heterogeneous systems. Software available from tensorflow.org.

Almahasees, Z and Zakaryia Mustafa. 2017. Machine translation quality of Khalil Gibran's the Prophet. *AWEJ for translation & Literary Studies Volume*, 1.

Ba, Jimmy Lei, Jamie Ryan Kiros, and Geoffrey E Hinton. 2016. Layer normalization. *arXiv preprint arXiv:1607.06450*. Version 1.

Bahdanau, Dzmitry, Kyunghyun Cho, and Yoshua Bengio. 2015. Neural machine translation by jointly learning to align and translate. In *Proceedings of the International Conference on Learning Representations (ICLR)*, May.

Besacier, Laurent and Lane Schwartz. 2015. Automated translation of a literary work: a pilot study. In *Proceedings of the Fourth Workshop on Computational Linguistics for Literature*, pages 114–122.

Cap, Fabienne, Ina Rösiger, and Jonas Kuhn. 2015. A pilot experiment on exploiting translations for literary studies on Kafka's "Verwandlung". In *Proceedings of the Fourth Workshop on Computational Linguistics for Literature*, pages 48–57, Denver, Colorado, USA, June. Association for Computational Linguistics.

Costa, Ângela, Wang Ling, Tiago Luís, Rui Correia, and Luísa Coheur. 2015. A linguistically motivated taxonomy for machine translation error analysis. *Machine Translation*, 29(2):127–161.

Flanagan, Mary. 1994. Error classification for MT evaluation. In *Technology Partnerships for Crossing the Language Barrier: Proceedings of the First Conference of the Association for Machine Translation in the Americas*, pages 65–72.

Genzel, Dmitriy, Jakob Uszkoreit, and Franz Och. 2010. "poetic" statistical machine translation: Rhyme and meter. In *Proceedings of the 2010 Conference on Empirical Methods in Natural Language Processing*, pages 158–166, Cambridge, MA, October. Association for Computational Linguistics.

Ghazvininejad, Marjan, Yejin Choi, and Kevin Knight. 2018. Neural poetry translation. In *Proceedings of the 2018 Conference of the North American Chapter of the Association for Computational Linguistics: Human Language Technologies, Volume 2 (Short Papers)*, pages 67–71.

He, Kaiming, Xiangyu Zhang, Shaoqing Ren, and Jian Sun. 2016. Deep residual learning for image recognition. In *2016 IEEE Conference on Computer Vision and Pattern Recognition, CVPR 2016, Las Vegas, NV, USA, June 27-30, 2016*, pages 770–778.

Kingma, Diederik P. and Jimmy Ba. 2015. Adam: A method for stochastic optimization. In *Proceedings of the International Conference on Learning Representations (ICLR)*, San Diego, CA, USA, May.

Korotkova, Elizaveta, Maksym Del, and Mark Fishel. 2018. Monolingual and cross-lingual zero-shot style transfer. *arXiv preprint arXiv:1808.00179*.

Kudo, Taku and John Richardson. 2018. Sentencepiece: A simple and language independent subword tokenizer and detokenizer for neural text processing. In *Proceedings of the 2018 Conference on Empirical Methods in Natural Language Processing: System Demonstrations*, pages 66–71.

Matusov, Evgeny, Patrick Wilken, Parnia Bahar, Julian Schamper, Pavel Golik, Albert Zeyer, Joan Albert Silvestre-Cerda, Adria Martınez-Villaronga, Hendrik Pesch, and Jan-Thorsten Peter. 2018. Neural speech translation at AppTek. In *International Workshop on Spoken Language Translation*.

Moryossef, Amit, Roee Aharoni, and Yoav Goldberg. 2019. Filling gender & number gaps in neural machine translation with black-box context injection. *arXiv preprint arXiv:1903.03467*.

Papineni, Kishore, Salim Roukos, Todd Ward, and Wei-Jing Zhu. 2002. BLEU: a Method for Automatic Evaluation of Machine Translation. In *Proceedings of the 41st Annual Meeting of the Association for Computational Linguistics*, pages 311–318, Philadelphia, Pennsylvania, USA, July.

Pereyra, Gabriel, George Tucker, Jan Chorowski, Lukasz Kaiser, and Geoffrey E. Hinton. 2017. Regularizing neural networks by penalizing confident output distributions. *CoRR*, abs/1701.06548.

Popović, Maja and Hermann Ney. 2011. Towards automatic error analysis of machine translation output. *Computational Linguistics*, 37(4):657–688.

Rabinovich, Ella, Shachar Mirkin, Raj Nath Patel, Lucia Specia, and Shuly Wintner. 2016. Personalized machine translation: Preserving original author traits. *arXiv preprint arXiv:1610.05461*.

Sennrich, Rico, Barry Haddow, and Alexandra Birch. 2016a. Improving neural machine translation models with monolingual data. pages 86–96, August.

Sennrich, Rico, Barry Haddow, and Alexandra Birch. 2016b. Neural machine translation of rare words with subword units. In *Proceedings of the 54th Annual Meeting of the Association for Computational Linguistics, ACL 2016, August 7-12, 2016, Berlin, Germany, Volume 1: Long Papers*.

Snover, Matthew, Bonnie Dorr, Richard Schwartz, Linnea Micciulla, and John Makhoul. 2006. A Study of Translation Edit Rate with Targeted Human Annotation. In *Proceedings of the 7th Conference of the Association for Machine Translation in the Americas*, pages 223–231, Cambridge, Massachusetts, USA, August.

Srivastava, Nitish, Geoffrey E. Hinton, Alex Krizhevsky, Ilya Sutskever, and Ruslan Salakhutdinov. 2014. Dropout: a simple way to prevent neural networks from overfitting. *Journal of Machine Learning Research*, 15(1):1929–1958.

Tiedemann, Jörg. 2012. Parallel data, tools and interfaces in OPUS. In *LREC*, volume 2012, pages 2214–2218.

Toral, Antonio and Andy Way. 2018. What level of quality can neural machine translation attain on literary text? In *Translation Quality Assessment*, pages 263–287. Springer.

Vaswani, Ashish, Noam Shazeer, Niki Parmar, Jakob Uszkoreit, Llion Jones, Aidan N Gomez, Łukasz Kaiser, and Illia Polosukhin. 2017. Attention is all you need. In *Advances in Neural Information Processing Systems*, pages 5998–6008.

Voigt, Rob and Dan Jurafsky. 2012. Towards a literary machine translation: The role of referential cohesion. In *Proceedings of the NAACL-HLT 2012 Workshop on Computational Linguistics for Literature*, pages 18–25.

Wang, Longyue, Zhaopeng Tu, Andy Way, and Qun Liu. 2017. Exploiting cross-sentence context for neural machine translation. *arXiv preprint arXiv:1704.04347*.

Zeyer, Albert, Tamer Alkhouli, and Hermann Ney. 2018. RETURNN as a generic flexible neural toolkit with application to translation and speech recognition. In *Proceedings of ACL 2018, Melbourne, Australia, July 15-20, 2018, System Demonstrations*, pages 128–133.

Using Intergaelic to pre-translate and subsequently post-edit a sci-fi novel from Scottish Gaelic to Irish

Eoin P. Ó Murchú
Research conducted at UCD, Belfield, Éire
Currently: PhD Student NUI Maynooth
Cill Dara
Éire
epomurchu@gmail.com

Abstract

In this paper I describe how I used Intergaelic, an ad-hoc hybrid machine translation (MT) system, to pre-translate a novel and subsequently post-edit the resulting MT output.[1] One of the central themes in the novel is the increasingly central role of technology in society. Thus this experiment can be viewed as a metatextual translation, whereby translation is aided by one of the themes present in the material being translated. I examine whether the translation provided by the MT system reached a basic standard that would reduce overall time for translation, and by how much. I examine the process of post-editing (PE) and how it differs from translation from scratch. I compare text generated by Intergaelic with that generated by widely available MT systems. I examine areas of weakness in this use of Intergaelic. I explore what elements remain the reserve of the human translator. I describe translating the entire novel using this method and how the author and publishers responded to the process of translation. I examine possible criticisms of this approach and the future of MT and PE in literary translation.

1 Intergaelic (IG)

Intergaelic was initially created by Kevin Scannell as an Irish-language standardising tool (for texts predating the standard language of *An Caighdeán Oifigiúil*, 1958) (Scannell, 2015). It was subsequently redesigned as an MT system for gisting of material in Scottish Gaelic (GD) for Irish-language speakers (2 closely related languages). IG is based on a corpus of 2.1 million words. This is relatively small compared to corpora available for major language pairs, but likely represents a significant percentage of all bilingual texts for this language pair. I used IG as an ad-hoc translation machine as I predicted that it would aid faster translation. IG is both rule-based and statistical-based. In relation to rules certain clusters of letters are changed, 'sg' to 'sc', (as in 'sgian' to 'scian') and 'chd' to 'cht' as in 'seacht' and 'seachd'. While neural MT has improved greatly in recent years approaches that use probability remain superior in the case of languages that lack a large amount of parallel texts.

Concern about the quality of MT for all languages, particularly around Google translate (GT) remains, despite significant improvements in recent iterations. Readers of Irish (GA) have even been acutely disappointed to find that certain books available online are the result of unedited MT. A poorly translated

[1] IG is available at http://www.intergaelic.com/gd-ga/trans/

copy of the Communist Manifesto is available.[2] While neural MT has improved greatly the improvement has been less marked for under-resourced languages. IG has the benefit of working with closely related languages.

I used IG in the present study as a tool to aid the speed of translation. An expertise in the source and target language are necessary. The accusation most commonly levelled against translation from English to Irish that is perceived to be of a poor quality is influence from the source language. IG cannot be accused of such influence as it contains only GA and GD. While the inner workings of GT are not entirely clear it seems that English is still often used as an intermediary step even when translating between major languages.

2 Air Cuan Dubh Drilseach (ACDD)

The novel in question is Tim Armstrong's *Air Cuan Dubh Drilseach* (Armstrong, 2013) the first hard sci-fi novel in GD.[3] The novel was awarded the Saltire Society First Book of the Year Award in 2013 and Scot Lit Fest named it one of the 5 most important novels in GD in 2016. The book outsold all GD books sold in the 2 years previous to its publication.[4] A sequel to the novel is currently being serialised in the GD literary magazine STEALL. Though Irish has a long history of sci-fi with *Cuairt ar an nGealaigh* appearing in 1923 and highlights such as Cathal Ó Sándair's *Captaen Spéirling* of the 1960's we have seen relatively little of the genre in Irish literature more recently (Mac Craith, 1923) (Ó Sándair, 1960).

3 Metatextual translation

ACDD describes a struggle against a supercapitalist society in which technology, particularly a fusion of AI and human intelligence, plays a central role. As IG is a basic AI my translation of the novel can be viewed as a *metatextual translation* of the novel whereby one of the central themes of the work is used to translate the work itself.[5] This causes us to ask an interesting question, what else could be viewed as metatextual translation? What other themes might be used as methods to translate literary works?

4 Comparison of Approaches

I conducted some tests to compare the quality, speed and difficulties with the various approaches. I initially translated sections of the novel from scratch. I then pre-translated the novel with IG and subsequently edited the IG output. In both cases I aimed for a solid first draft, one that I was happy with on rereading in which the translation flowed and which showed no errors.[6] The quality of the IG translation varied from sentences that needed no correction to others that needed to be rewritten entirely. I include below a comparison of sentences from the text.

Source text GD	Translation from scratch	IG output	IG output post-edited
Bha an triùir nan suidhe ann an cearcall cruinn an taca teine fhosgailte: Sàl,	Bhí an triúr suite i gciorcal timpeall ar thine oscailte: Sàl,	Bhí an triúr ina suí i gciorcal cruinn an taca tine oscailte: Sàl,	Bhí an triúr acu ina suí i gciorcal cruinn timpeall ar thine bheag: Sàl,

[2] https://www.amazon.com/Forogra-Cumannach-Communist-Manifesto-2016-06-14/dp/B01NAOH7HP/ref=sr_1_2?keywords=communist+manifesto+irish&qid=1564356902&s=gateway&sr=8-2 For those looking for an accurate translation see *Clár na Comharsheilbhe: forógra Pháirtí na gCumannach* (Marx, 1986).

[3] The title can be translated as *On a Glittering Dark Sea.*

[4] Information from Comhairle nan Leabhraichean | The Gaelic Books Council.

[5] The term 'metatextual translation' has been used previously in other contexts but I feel it is fitting to describe my approach in the present study. My search for a term was further complicated by the fact that the terms 'metathematic translation' and 'metatranslation', which might also suit this role, have also previously been used in other contexts.

[6] This step of the study is limited in as far as translation and analysis performed was done by myself and was not blinded. In future, translations could be analysed by an independent professional translator.

Rìosa agus Sabhair, agus iad aig beul na h-oidhche air a' ghealaich bhig, Roghail, a bha na dachaigh dhaibh.	Rìosa agus Sabhair sa chlapsholas ar an ngealach bheag, Roghail, a mbaile.	Rìosa agus Sabhair, agus iad ag béal na hoíche ar an ngealach bhig, Roghail, a bhí na baile dóibh.	Rìosa agus Sabhair, é ina chlapsholas ar an ngealach bheag, Roghail, a bhí mar bhaile acu.

Translation from scratch resulted in a freer translation in which the word order and sentence structure is more varied compared to the source text. The post-edited IG output follows the structure of the source text more closely. Translation is more long-winded at times and there appears to be a tendency to explicitation, information that was implicit in the source text has been added in the translated text. Translation from scratch is shorter for this sentence, likely due to the fact that I as translator wasn't primed with certain structures by IG. The IG process more closely followed the structure of the IG text and therefore the source text.

Source text GD	Translation from scratch	Raw IG output	IG output post-edited
Gu h-àrd, bha a' phlanaid dhearg, Na Hasta, a' coimhead sìos air an triùir mar shùil mhòir anns na speuran.	Lastuas bhí an pláinéad, Na Hasta, ag breathnú anuas ar an triúr mar a bheadh súil mhór spéire ann.	Go hard, bhí an phláinéad dhearg, Na Hasta, ag breathnú síos ar an triúr mar shúil mhóir sna spéartha.	Bhí an pláinéad dearg, Na Hasta, in airde ag breathnú anuas ar an triúr mar a bheadh súil mhór sna spéartha.

The raw IG output is intelligible and largely grammatically correct. A relatively high level of GA and GD ability would be required to translate at this level. Some elements remain untranslated such as 'an taca'. Older dative forms remain and gender is not corrected in translation. IG output post-editing, while differing from translation from scratch, does share many similarities. One of the issues I recognised, as MT had a role in the loop, was that I felt as a translator that I had to be hypervigilant to ensure any clangers caused by MT would not end up in the final translation. This concern remains despite subsequent drafts and was not felt in translation from scratch.

5 BLEU score

I decided to analyse the BLEU scores of the various translations generated.[7] A BLEU score assesses how similar the raw MT output is to a from scratch translation. The score is correlated with human assessment. It is not based on language but matches words, and strings of words. It is in common use and has been described as objective. A BLEU score of 0 means that 0% of the text is similar to one translated by a human. 100 means that 100% similar to human translation. A BLEU score of over 30% is generally recognised as intelligible and 40-45% and above is recognised as the threshold for PE.

The test passages translated in *ACDD* had a BLEU score of 35%. Despite not reaching the generally recognised level required my analysis found that the process of using IG and PE was faster compared to translation from scratch. This might relate to the fact that GA and GD are closely related languages. We must also remember that BLEU has its limitations. A highly accomplished translation might get a low score if it is very dissimilar to a given human translation. IG can prime the human translator with certain structures that are acceptable yet different to structures that the human translator would have generated from scratch. While GT has improved significantly in recent years a translation of these test passages done by GT in May 2019 was significantly worse than translations done by IG.

[7] I used Asiya developed by the Universitat Politècnica de Catalunya and available at http://asiya.lsi.upc.edu/

6 Productivity Comparison

I next aimed to find out whether IG and post-editing changed the speed of translation. I translated sections of 300 words from three chapters.[8]

Comparison of translation time 1 (chapter 1)	Test 2 (chapter 2)	Test 3 (chapter 3)
20.39 minutes (MT)	16.20 (MT)	22.15 (MT)
24.49 (translation from scratch)	32.10 (from scratch)	28.03 (from scratch)

IG and PE were 31% faster compared to translation from scratch. I must mention that processing in IG took a certain amount of time but as the entire text was processed in one go, the time spent per passage was negligible overall.[9] It must be noted that the time spent in both translation approaches was spent very differently. With MT and PE less time was spent typing as most of the words required were had already been provided by IG. It was often easiest to move words around, to delete words or add a word. More time was also spent rereading the translation to ensure it flowed.

7 Criticism of IG

Translating from scratch results in more natural Irish, in these initial drafts at least. As I was starting with a blank page in translation from scratch, I moved from the word order and sentence structure and length of the source text more frequently. I felt that it might have been easy to leave sentences created by IG in the translation if they appeared to reach an acceptable standard, where I might have translated them differently if I had not been primed by IG. As basic as IG may sometimes seem, it recognised the correct sense of a polysemous word that initially was missed by this translator. The word 'dealanach' I initially understood as relating to 'lighting', IG provided the correct sense of 'electronic'.

8 Elements where IG fails

Many elements remain the reserve of the human translator. These included; proper nouns, chapter titles, regional accents, neologisms and interjections. The corpus behind IG lacks the data to deal with some of these issues and named-entity recognition is a recognised weakness of MT.

Some elements relating to the structural differences of both languages presented a challenge. Tense in GA and GD does not map exactly to each other. The structure most commonly used to represent the passive voice of GD is the Irish autonomous verb whereby structures such as 'Chaidh an talla a thogail…' are translated by 'Tógadh an balla'.

Sometimes multiple translations of a single source word were given, the words 'pasáiste' and 'halla' were given for 'trannsa' in the same paragraph. Alternatively sometimes a single translation was given for multiple source terms. 'Bhí an duine cibirniteach gnóthach gnóthach' was given as a translation for '[...]trang, dripeil' in GD. Polysemous words such as 'clár' represented a challenge.

Faux amis were a particular challenge, perhaps due to fact that GA and GD are closely related languages. Such words, despite being faux amis, often had semantic overlap and inappropriate use might be easily missed in post-editing.[10]

9 Acceptability of literary MT

MT software is currently the industry standard used for pragmatic translation of, for instance, info booklets, reports and textbooks. MT along with PE has been shown to be up to 42.9% faster and has been shown to increase quality in

[8] This part of the research is limited in that it was not blinded. I did however ensure that I translated under the same conditions in both approaches, including performing the same amount of warm-up translation before translating passages and alternating which approach was used first.

[9] Many thanks to Kevin Scannell for assistance with this.

[10] The following examples were noted; 'geal' and 'bán', 'luath' and 'tapa, 'an té' and 'an bhean', 'mullach' and 'díon', 'lorg' and 'aimsiú'.

some cases. The subtleties of literature are of course more challenging. A project to translate Camus' *L'Étranger* to English and Italian, found that the result with Italian was better. (Toral et al 2015). A significant amount of editing was required. But if the translation is finished more speedily and of the same quality is it not worth it? We know that globally translation demand is increasing. A script for a Harry Potter play reached the top of the bestseller charts in France in 2016 despite the fact that it was in English (Agence France-Presse, 2016). In an increasingly globalised world, turnaround time for translation will get even shorter. MT might also represent a way for traditionally poorly-paid literary translators to increase output.

What will happen to translators in this digital age of ever-improving MT? [11] The role is likely to change to that of literary post-editor. While such approaches are more likely to happen in popular fiction acceptance might take longer for perceived high-literature. I suspect that MT and PE are likely in use in some genres of literature already. My use of IG in this project likely resulted in thousands or tens of thousands of differences compared to the text that I would have translated from scratch. If two professional translators were to translate a given text of this length, you would likely see even more differences. I hold that my use of MT and PE as above is acceptable. I am concerned, however, that this approach would ultimately result in the demotion of human intellectual labour. I see no reason why MT alone should not ultimately be superior to human literary translation.

10 Response of the author and publishers to translation approach

The novel is currently being edited and a publisher intends to publish it. The publisher has a positive view of the project. 'This is an extremely interesting [project] and we would of course be very interested in publishing such a book.'[12] The text as post-edited by myself will be edited as a translated Irish text. This process would have also happened in the case of a scratch translation submitted to the publisher. Another publisher accepted the translation approach but decided against publishing the book on other grounds.[13]

Although the present publisher had doubts about the process they were assuaged by the fact that the MT text would be post-edited by myself. The editor would be looking at the end product rather than the process. '[I]f a machine carries out preliminary work on a document that comes before me, it does not necessarily make any difference to me - I am only looking at the final product and not at the process.'[14]

The author was extremely positive, perhaps unsurprisingly for someone interested in the genre of sci-fi. 'As an author, and especially as someone who writes science fiction, your translation project was very appealing to me. Machine translation suits the theme of the novel very well, as well as the practical benefits. For me it will be interesting to see how the reader will accept it, knowing that a basic (AI) machine was involved in creating the text they are reading. But I am not concerned; I am looking forward to it. It is thought-provoking.'[15]

11 Conclusion

I hold that IG and PE is an acceptable translation approach for a sci-fi novel. IG aided me in translating the novel 31% faster than a

[11] I might mention that as a tutor in translation in an Irish third level institution in 2019 I noticed that GT outperformed all but one of approximately 60 third year students in translation of a short pragmatic passage from English to Irish.

[12] Translated from a personal email. 'Tá sé sin thar a bheith spéisiúil agus, dar ndóigh, bheadh an-spéis againn ina leithéide de leabhar a fhoilsiú'

[13] A previous translation from Scottish Gaelic published by the publishers had sold poorly.

[14] Translated from a personal email. '[M]á thagann cáipéis faoi mo bhráidse a raibh meaisín in úsáid leis an réamhobair a dhéanamh uirthi, ní gá go ndéanfadh sé aon difríocht domsa — is ar an obair chríochnúil amháin a bheas mise ag breathnú agus ní ar an bpróiséas.'

[15] Translated from a personal email. 'Mar ùghdar, agus gu sònraichte mar chuideigin a sgrìobhas ficsean-saidheans, bha an tionnsgnadh eadar-theangachaidh agad gu math tarraingeach dhomh. Tha mi a' smaoineachadh gu bheil eadar-theangachadh innealta a' freagairt glè mhath air cuspair na nobhail, a bharrachd air na buannachdan practaigeach a thig na lùib. Dhomhsa, bidh e gu math inntinneach faicinn ciamar a ghabhas an leughadair ris, is fios aca gun robh tùr innealta (AI) bunasach an sàs ann an cruthachadh an teacsa a bhios iad a' leughadh. Ach chan eil eagal orm; tha mi a' dèanamh fiughair ris. Bidh e smaoineachail.'

translation from scratch. In sections of the text over 50% of the tokens remaining in the third draft had been provided by IG. I found that the standard was similar to translation from scratch. I recognised some issues with IG which are tractable and resolved in the PE step.

I recognise that a principled philosophical stance against MT and PE might be warranted as MT is likely to change the role of translators to editors and ultimately take up their role entirely. The translation approach was acceptable to the author and to two publishers.

In relation to further research a closer and more objective analysis of the varying approaches would provide a better understanding of the process. A blinded comparison with translation by an independent professional translator along with a review of my post-edited translations and translations from scratch would add to the strength of findings above. IG also exists for Manx Gaelic, the possibility to translate from that language could be examined in future. The approach outlined above might initially be more acceptable in translation of news articles and pragmatic text.

References;

Agence France-Presse. 2016. Harry Potter and the Cursed Child play tops French bestseller list – in English. The Guardian. 11 August.

Armstrong, Tim. 2013. *Air Cuan Dubh Drilseach*, CLÀR.

Coughlin, Deborah A. 2003. Correlating Automated and Human Assessments of Machine Translation Quality, Association for Machine Translation in the Americas.

Mac Craith, Mícheál. 1923. *Cuairt ar an nGealaigh*. Fáinne an Lae.

Martinez, Lorena Guerra. 2004. Human translation versus machine translation and full post-editing of raw machine translation output, *International Journal of Translation* 16(2): 81-113.

Marx, Karl & Friedrich Engels. 1986. *Clár na Comharsheilbhe: forógra Pháirtí na gCumannach*. Páirtí Cumannach na hÉireann, Baile Átha Cliath.

Oifig an tSoláthair. 1958. *Gramadach na Gaeilge agus Litriú na Gaeilge – An Caighdeán Oifigiúil* Baile Átha Cliath, Oifig an tSoláthair.

Parra Escartín, Carla & Arcedillo, Manuel. 2015. Living on the edge: productivity gain thresholds in machine translation evaluation metrics. 46-56.

Ó Sándair, Cathal. 1960. *Captaen Spéirling agus an Phláinéad do Phléasc,* Baile Átha Cliath, Oifig an tSoláthair.

Scannell, Kevin, 2015. Eadar-Ghaeilg: Scottish and Manx Gaelic resources for Irish speakers, University of Notre Dame, 5 October.

Toral, Antonio & Way, Andy. 2015. Machine-assisted translation of literary text: A case study. *Translation Spaces*. 4. 240-267

Would MT kill creativity in literary retranslation?

Mehmet Şahin
Izmir University of Economics / Department of Translation and Interpretation
rbsmsahin@gmail.com

Sabri Gürses
Independent Scholar
sgurses@gmail.com

Abstract

The increasing number of retranslations and wider availability of their texts on the Internet is expected to create a positive impact on MT systems by producing more matches. Yet, we argue that retranslations conducted using MT would differ from those completed without any recourse to MT in terms of creative solutions. This paper aims to discuss the possible effects of MT on retranslation of literary texts with a focus on creativity. 21 fourth-year T&I students translated two excerpts from Robinson Crusoe into Turkish, one with, and one without the help of an online MT service. We included the analysis of four different translations of the same text available on the market, in terms of creativity. Analysis of solutions produced for 252 translation units suggests that the use of MT is likely to hinder creativity for novice translators for English-Turkish language pair.

1 Introduction

Retranslation requires high level of creativity and originality. Although the range and volume of digitally-available and copyrightless literary works is growing, the classics remain the most attractive texts for translators and publishers, and thus the most frequently subject to retranslation in many contexts.

The rise of artificial intelligence (AI) and dominance of high-quality machine translation (MT) and computer-aided translation (CAT) tools in the translation profession brings the need to reconsider the assessment of retranslations of literary works. The digitization and online availability of the texts of earlier translations as processable data for MT providers is likely to encourage retranslators to have recourse to such tools.

In this paper, we report on a small-scale experiment to demonstrate the potential effects on creativity of using MT for retranslation. We explore two possible effects of MT. On the one hand, we can argue that in retranslations, it is desirable to focus on the more lexically and syntactically complex structures in the source text, rather than the relatively easier parts. In this case, using MT might give translators freedom to engage in a more intense focus on such key sections of the text, and thus boost creativity. On the other hand, MT is likely to inhibit translators, particularly novices, by appearing to make the translation process more straightforward than it actually is. This approach risks undermining critical thinking process, and constraining the capacity to find creative solutions to translation problems.

Furthermore, the use of MT in literary retranslation raises another issue explored in studies, plagiarism in translations. The widespread use of MT is likely to hinder detection of plagiaristic elements in retranslation, since it can pave the way for a new mode of "translation", namely *transcollage*. We discuss this recent trend, based on the current examples, and the possible repercussions of MT-driven retranslation.

2 Background

In the current study, we investigate the level of creativity in MT-supported retranslations. This brings into focus several key concepts, such as retranslation, plagiarism, and the use of MT for literary translation, and creativity in retranslation.

2.1 Retranslation

Retranslation is defined as "either the act of translating a work that has previously been translated into the same language, or the result of such an act, i.e. the retranslated text itself."

(Gürçağlar, 2009). Retranslation in literature adds value to, repairs and competes with the earlier efforts, and through this evolutionary process creates a genealogy and history of translation. In a retranslation, as well as seeking the translator's personal voice, one may feel the need to understand the retranslator's agenda. Without such a new voice, perspective or agenda, it may even be difficult to describe it as a translation. In most cases, the repetitive or plagiaristic elements are clearly seen in the text.

2.2 Plagiarism

Plagiarism in translation has been a topic of discussion for the last two decades in various contexts, especially in Turkey (Turell, 2004; Gürses, 2007; 2008; 2011). This phenomenon was investigated in a two-year scientific project funded by The Scientific and Technological Research Council of Turkey (Şahin, Duman & Gürses, 2015a). One of the findings of the project was that of 28 different Turkish retranslations of Robinson Crusoe, only two showed satisfactory level of originality. The boom in retranslations of classics in Turkey is strongly linked to profit-oriented publishing policies fed by plagiarism (Şahin, Duman & Gürses, 2015b). Currently, two possible approaches to detect plagiarism in retranslations are document collusion programs, such as *CopyCatch Investigator* ®, and qualitative analysis of translations. Yet, the use of MT for literary translation is expected to pose new challenges.

2.3 MT for literary texts

The use of MT for literary translation has become a topic of discussion in translation circles. The view that MT cannot be used for literary texts is now being challenged.

Moorkens et al. (2018), in their study investigating post-editing of literary texts, concluded that "all participants prefer to translate from scratch, mostly due to the freedom to be creative without the constraints of segment-level segmentation, those with less experience find the MT suggestions useful." The use of MT for English-Turkish language pair also was investigated in several studies for different text genres, including literary texts with SMT paradigm (Şahin 2014, Şahin & Dungan 2014). Findings emphasized low quality of MT output was quite low in those experiments and the negative attitude of translators to using MT in the translation process, especially for literary texts.

2.4 Creativity in retranslations

Retranslations are expected to offer the readers novel and better solutions, thus require retranslators to show more creativity, which "is most usefully defined as something which happens in translation and is demanded of translators." (Sullivan, 2013). Sullivan also argues that "[a]lthough literary texts are by no means the only texts which prompt creative responses, they are an important resource for promoting student creativity and language sensitivity." (2013)

Paul Kussmaul (2000), one of the leading scholars focusing on creativity in translation, argues that "[s]cenic visualisations [...] contribute to the novelty of a translation and help make it a creative product." The question of increasing use of MT in translation could contribute to creative solutions has not yet been answered. However, recent studies touch upon the issue peripherally, and provide empirical evidence.

In one of those studies, Toral (2019) investigated whether there is evidence of post-editese, and how PE differs from HT, in a corpus of news articles for different language pairs. By looking at the so-called 'translation universals' (Baker, 1993), Toral found that "PEs tend to be simpler and more normalised and to have a higher degree of interference from the source text than HTs.".

Stressing that "We need to help translators expand their creative repertoires of translation strategies.", Robinson (1998) disassociates creativity from convergent thinking which entails "avoiding errors by narrowing in on the most conventional solution and refusing to take, or even to contemplate taking, risks — and enjoyment".

In our study, we define creative translation as solutions that go beyond literal translation and differ from the MT solution. In line with these considerations, we addressed the following questions:

- How does MT-aided retranslation affect novice translators' creativity in literary texts for the English-Turkish language pair?
- What is the opinion of novice translators in regard to the use of MT in literary retranslation?

3 Method

We conducted a small-scale experiment with 21 fourth-year translation and interpreting (T&I) students following a course on literary translation, and with some experience in post-editing. They translated into Turkish two excerpts (142 words and 145 words in length) from Robinson Crusoe. This classic has been frequently retranslated (about 30 times) into Turkish in the last three decades. Some of these retranslations are, partly or fully, available on the Internet.

The participants were divided into two groups. The first group translated the first excerpt using Internet resources on an online word-processing program, and the second excerpt by post-editing the Google Translate output, again using any Internet resources. The second group completed the translation task in the opposite order in terms of mode; that is the first excerpt was post-editing and the second was unaided human translation. The maximum time allowed for each task was one hour. Upon completion, the participants also wrote a short paragraph expressing their opinion about MT-aided and unaided literary translation.

Each translation was transferred to a Google Spreadsheet, and in each translation six translation units were selected for analysis in each mode (HT and MT+PE), according to where creativity was expected to come into play.

3.1 Sample Text

I was born in the year 1632, in the city of York, **of a good family, though not of that country**, my father being a foreigner of Bremen who settled first at Hull.

He got a good estate by merchandise and, leaving off his trade, lived afterward at York, from whence he had married my mother, whose relations were named Robinson, a very good family in that country, and from whom I was called Robinson Kreutznaer; **but by the usual corruption of words in England** we are now called, nay, we call ourselves, and write our name "Crusoe" and so my companions always called me.

I had two elder brothers, **one of which was lieutenant colonel to an English regiment of foot in Flanders**, formerly commanded by the famous Colonel Lockhart, and was killed at the battle near Dunkirk against the Spaniards.

What became of my second brother, I never knew, **any more than my father and my mother did know what was become of me**.

Being the third son of the family, **and not bred to any trade**, my head began to be filled very early with rambling thoughts.

My father, who was **very ancient, had given me a competent share of learning**, as far as house-education and a country free school generally go, and designed me for the law; but I would be satisfied with nothing but going to sea; and my inclination to this led me so strongly **against the will, nay, the commands of my father**, and against all the entreaties and persuasions of my mother and other friends, that there seemed to be something fatal in that propensity of nature, **tending directly to the life of misery which was to befall me**.

3.2 Analysis

We categorized translation solutions as follows:

- literal translation
- MT solution (literal, creative, or erroneous translation)
- creative solution (going beyond literal translation)
- undertranslation (not conveying the message fully)
- mistranslation (conveying the message incorrectly)
- untranslated (omitting the whole unit)

We only used four of the published translations: the first translation, and three retranslations. We analyzed the translations in terms of the expressions in bold, a total of 252 translation units. We acknowledge that some categories can overlap; for example, a literal translation solution can overlap with solutions found in previous translations. We coded each solution according to the categories listed above.

4 Results

The analysis of student translations based on MT solutions and previous translations provided results regarding the effect of using MT in literary translation on creativity.

4.1 Initial observations

MT output produced by Google Translate seems consistent with unaided translation outputs (student translations as well as retranslations already available in the market) in terms of sustaining-adapting words; neither output localizes. For example, the human translator and retranslators have not focused on the readers' perspective: 'Flanders' is transferred unchanged without giving the reader *Flamand / Flemish* context. Only two students in HT mode noted this and localized the word, whereas MT output in French does this automatically.

MT output also seems to present translations more faithful to the source text structure. Professional as well student translators tend to divide long sentences into parts, unlike MT. The tendency to keep the form of the original may be a sign and test of creativity from the perspective of the translator; so translational strategies correlate with creativity.

9 out of 12 translation units were translated by MT incorrectly and one translation unit was undertranslated. Other two translation units were translated accurately, one literally and one creatively.

4.2 Student translations

Time spent for translation both in HT and MT+PE modes was very close (See Table 1). Although the participants spent almost as much time as the other mode adjusting the MT output (see Table 1), in most instances they preferred to maintain MT output. The number of mistranslations was high in both modes, mostly due to comprehension problems. The participants did not check earlier published translations during the experiment.

As can be seen in Charts 1-3, the percentage of creative solutions that the participants produced is higher in the HT mode. In the MT+PE mode, the participants preferred to rely on MT solutions, whether literal or erroneous, to a considerable extent. Approximately, 23% of the translation solutions by Group 1 and 59% of Group 2 originated from the MT output, which was obtained through Google Translate. We observed overlapping solutions by MT, retranslators, and student translators as well. For example, the word "ancient" is translated into Turkish inaccurately not only by Google Translate, but also by retranslators and students, except for one. The translation unit "I was born" is translated as "doğdum" by MT and this solution is kept by all of the participants in MT+PE mode, whereas only two out of 10 participants used this solution in HT mode. Only about 7% of translation solutions produced by the student translators were exactly similar to those in earlier published translations included in our study.

4.3 Student views

Only two out of 21 participants found MT+PE more efficient, the remainder complained about the difficulty of post-editing and stated that they preferred translating from scratch. This was mostly due to the complex sentence structures in the source text. Three of the comments by the participants are as follows:

G2-S5 (Group2-Student5)
It took the same time for me to post-edit a MT and to translate a similar text on my own. Machine translation fails to successfully translate such complex sentence structures, and there seems to be many mistakes in the MT, I would have preferred to translate the first part myself, upon seeing the MT. Translating on my own, for me was rather easier when compared to post-editing, as MT often seemed to confuse me with both its word choices and sentence structure changes. I had to pay more attention to the text due to these elements. As for the translation process itself, I found the text to be complex on a similar level but very much enjoyed translating it since it was a literary translation and a challenge on its own.

G2-S8
Even though the post editing and translation processes took a similar amount of time for me, post editing process was more efficient and easier when we consider the translation of the text. Except for the long sentence in second paragraph, sentence structures were good enough, and I did not need to change sentence structures so much.

G2-S11
Even though there are some advances in MT systems, non-similar language pairs (e.g. Turkish and English in this case, as they are from different language families) still seem to be problematic for MT. Some words were translated incorrectly, and disentangling the mess caused by the lengthy sentences of the source text proved to be more challenging than making the translation from scratch.
The translation (and not MT) was easier, and I felt like I had more command over the process than in the first step of the assignment. As far as the time spent on each task is concerned, it seems plausible to think that long and complex sentences, in the current technical circumstances, should be handled by human translators rather than automated processes.

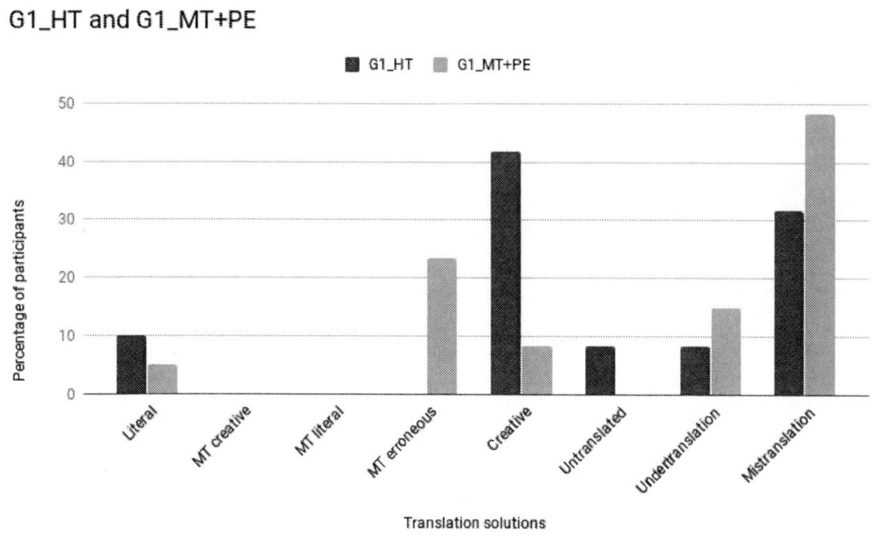

Chart 1. Translation solutions by Group 1 (n=10)

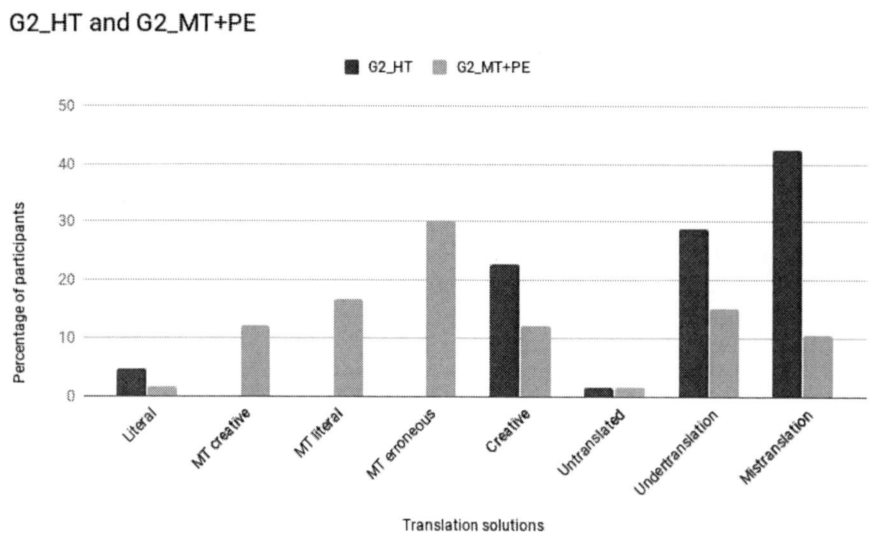

Chart 2. Translation solutions by Group 2 (n=11)

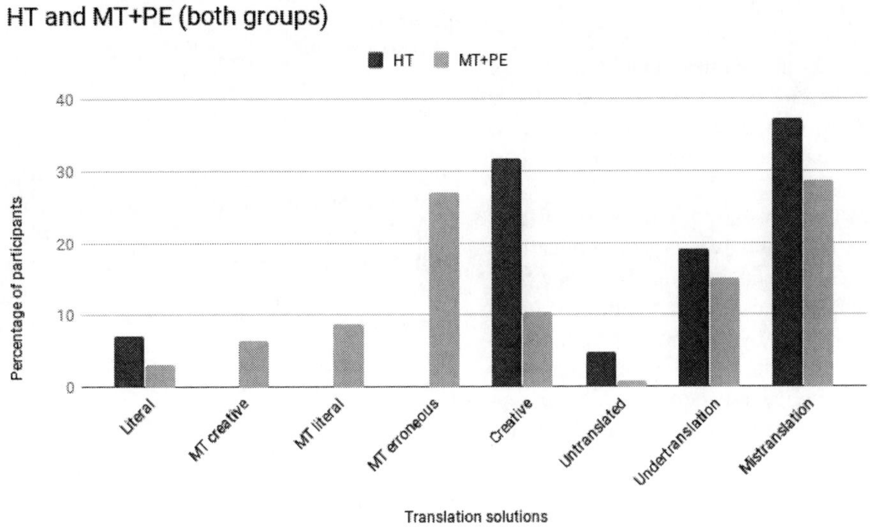

Chart 3. Translation solutions by all participants (n=21)

Table 1. Average time spent on translation tasks

	G1		G2	
	HT	MT+PE	HT	MT+PE
Average time spent in minutes	20.8	20	18.18	16.18

5 Conclusion

Our study focused on the question how the use of MT in translation of literary texts affects creativity. We used a qualitative analysis of a small set of data produced by fourth-year T&I students.

Toral (2019) warns that "the extensive use of PE rather than HT may have serious implications for the target language in the long term, for example that it becomes impoverished (simplification) and overly influenced by the source language (interference)." This finding is relevant to our study as well because novice translators are also susceptible to interference of source language due to literal solutions provided by MT services. In another relevant study, Vanmassenhove, Shterionov, and Way (2019) observed that "the process of MT causes a general loss in terms of lexical diversity and richness when compared to human-generated text."

Our findings generally corroborate Toral's (2019) and Vanmassenhove, Shterionov, and Way's (2019) findings that students created less original solutions with MT aid; and more original in non-MT mode . A parallel can be drawn with a driverless car: when controlled by humans, the number of routes expand, and safety is increased. We also found that novice translators had difficulty in analyzing complex sentence structures, and hence mistranslated the high number of units in our analysis. Yet, this might be due to time pressure, as they were limited to one hour to complete the translation task in a laboratory setting.

As Kussmaul (2000) states "We are faced here with a specific feature of creativity in translating, which at first sight seems to be a paradox. On the one hand translators can fulfil the requirement of novelty only if they move away from the source text; on the other hand, it may be more adequate for the overall purpose not to move very far from the source text and thus be less creative." (p. 124). In this regard, MT use seems to be an adequate choice because of the linearity it presents. Yet, literary translation, and retranslation in particular, requires creativity entailing novel solutions. Unlike the conclusion of Moorkens et al. (2018), our participants, relatively inexperienced, found MT suggestions rather unhelpful, as reported in their post-experiment reflections.

Our results suggest that assuming that MT to Turkish continues to develop, it will help the translator to produce more creative retranslations, and may help free the translator from laborious work and become more creative and open to experiment.

However, we argue that, even in its present state, using MT may help the translator 1) to check work, 2) or to create work by editing, 3) and to see her good and bad points. Nevertheless, starting with MT-editing may be time consuming, so probably own translations should be compared with the MT version. But if translators feel that it will be difficult to be creative, then they could start with MT version. We know that editors in publishing houses are uninterested in whether the text is human or MT, or even group work, they merely need a usable, original text from a human translator as named author who is legally responsible for the text.

But then, even if this is true for translation, in the case of retranslation, it becomes complex, as MT or HT may resemble other retranslations. Our experiment is important because it shows that, even though there exist several retranslations of a work, translations of greater creativity are possible in HT and even in MT. In fact, we may say that, if used wisely, MT becomes a tool for the retranslator in the same way as past HTs of the same text in the same language, and it is extremely likely that MT aid will eventually become as common as dictionaries are today.

One drawback in our investigation is that students have not yet achieved professionalism and professional attitudes, meaning they do not yet behave like professional translators in the field. In literary retranslation business, it is always a point of interest whether the retranslator considered other translations and whether there is any correlation with the current retranslation. This looking up and preliminary research process is in fact crucial if the republisher and retranslator intends to add value to the product; but in the Turkish case, our analysis of the published texts revealed no such an intention. The added value has been newness in translation alone, without new forewords by specialists in the field or footnotes to reveal the historical context. This shows that MT may add much value to the translation; for example, Google Translate has a pronunciation/reading tool, and words can be searched on the Internet for images, dictionary and encyclopedia entries. Yandex Translator has added previous Russian to English literary translations to its database, which are revealed if you try to translate from a Russian classic. As these tools evolve, they will probably either make retranslation unnecessary or make human retranslation evolve into a cyborg translation, in which the personal translation will be available for the consumer. In addition, we may be witnessing a shift from the question of whether the translator will use MT, to the question of whether MT will need a translator, and in the case of retranslation, the answer is, not necessarily.

But today, even though the translation from, say, Finnish to English has developed greatly (Robinson 2019), translations into Turkish still have to catch up, and this makes our analysis necessary. In the Turkish case, we need to be aware that there is a market for plagiarism in retranslations; these are produced with methods such as renewing, changing the words, syntax, and sometimes, collaging different translations, which we call *transcollaging*. The producer of plagiarism does not aim at better texts, although this is possible, but usually they aim only to hide resemblances. The problem here is to decide whether MT is consistently repeating the same translation, or whether it is evolving, changing every day and giving different solutions to different users. If the latter is the case, a plagiarist (or so-called translator) may use MT to get a literary retranslation without recourse to other human retranslations, and there will be nothing beyond an IP number to identify him. This is a problem for attention and our investigation, which reveals similarities among Crusoe retranslations, plagiarisms and student works must be borne in mind in future analyses.

We should note that the source text in our study contains structures and expressions that could pose challenges for translators, whether professional or student. MT use can be more helpful for relatively easier literary texts. Further experiments should be conducted with different texts, and as well as with professional translators. Finally, comparing different online MT services, such as Bing Translator and Yandex and other offline commercial systems, in addition to Google Translate, would enable us to better assess the potential of MT use for creativity in retranslation.

References

Baker, Mona. 1993. Corpus linguistics and translation studies: Implications and applications. Text and technology: In honour of John Sinclair, 233:250.

Gürses, Sabri. 2007. "İntihal Kültürü" [Culture of Plagiarism]. *Varlık 1194*: 9–16.

Gürses, Sabri. 2008. Çeşitli Örneklerle Çeviri İntihalleri [Plagiarism in Translation through Examples]. In *Proceedings of the Colloquium on Translation Ethics: Ethical Issues in Translation and in Translation Profession?* [Çeviri Etiği Toplantısı: Çeviri ve Çevirmenliğin Etik Sorunları]. İstanbul: Istanbul University Publications.

Gürses, Sabri. 2011. Translational Plagiarism: National History, Global Prospects. *Çeviribilim 4*: 6–7.

Kussmaul, Paul. 2000. Types of creative translating. Benjamins translation library, 39, 117-126.

Malmkjær, Kirsten. 2019. *Translation and Creativity*. New York and London: Routledge.

Moorkens, Joss, Toral, Antonio, Castilho, Sheila, and Andy Way. 2018. Translators' perceptions of literary post-editing using statistical and neural machine translation. *Translation Spaces*, *7*(2), 240-262.

Robinson, Douglas. 1998. 22 Theses on Translation. http://home.olemiss.edu/~djr/pages/writer/articles/html/22theses.html

Robinson, Douglas. 2019. *Nasıl Çevirmen Olunur.* Translated by Sabri Gürses. İstanbul: Çeviribilim.

Sullivan, Carol. 2013. Creativity. *Handbook of Translation Studies Volume 4*, pp. 42–46. John Benjamins Publishing Company.

Şahin, Mehmet. 2014. Using MT post-editing for translator training», *Tralogy* [En ligne], Tralogy II, Session 6 - Teaching around MT / Didactique, enseignement, apprentissage, mis à jour le : 25/08/2014,URL : http://lodel.irevues.inist.fr/tralogy/index.php?id=255

Şahin, Mehmet, and Nilgün Dungan. 2014. "Translation testing and evaluation: A study on methods and needs." *Translation & Interpreting* 6.2: 67-90.

Şahin, Mehmet, Duman, Derya, Gürses, Sabri, Kaleş, Damla, and David Woolls. 2018. "Toward an Empirical Methodology for Identifying Plagiarism in Retranslation." In *Perspectives on Retranslation: Ideology, Paratexts, Methods*, edited by Özlem Berk Albachten and Şehnaz Tahir Gürçağlar, 166-191. New York: Routledge.

Şahin, Mehmet, Duman, Derya, and Sabri Gürses. 2015a. *Plagiarism in Translation (Grant No: 112K388).* Final Report, Ankara: The Scientific and Technological Research Council of Turkey.

Şahin, Mehmet, Duman, Derya, and Sabri Gürses. 2015b. Big business of plagiarism under the guise of (re) translation: The case of Turkey. *Babel*, *61*(2), 193-218.

Tahir Gürçağlar, Şehnaz. (2009). Retranslation. In M. Baker, & G. Saldana (Eds.), *Routledge Encyclopedia of Translation Studies* (pp. 233-236). New York and London: Routledge.

Taivalkoski-Shilov, Kriistina (2018). Ethical issues regarding machine (-assisted) translation of literary texts. *Perspectives*, 1-15.

Toral, Antonio. 2019. Post-editese: an Exacerbated Translationese. *arXiv preprint arXiv:1907.00900.*

Toral, Antonio, and Andy Way. 2018. What level of quality can Neural Machine Translation attain on literary text?. In *Translation Quality Assessment* (pp. 263-287). Springer, Cham.

Turrell, Teresa M.. 2004. Textual kidnapping revisited: The case of plagiarism in literary translation. *International Journal of Speech, Language and the Law, 11*, 1–26.

Vanmassenhove, Eva, Dimitar Shterionov, and Andy Way. (2019). Lost in Translation: Loss and Decay of Linguistic Richness in Machine Translation. arXiv preprint arXiv:1906.12068.

Free indirect discourse: an insurmountable challenge for literary MT systems?

Kristiina Taivalkoski-Shilov[1]
School of Languages and Translation Studies
Koskenniemenkatu 4
20014, University of Turku
Finland
kristiina.taivalkoski-shilov@utu.fi

Abstract

This paper argues that an essential element affecting literary translation – the structure of narrative discourse – has been overlooked in research on literary MT systems so far. After a brief survey of basic concepts of structuralist narratology (Genette 1972), which are necessary for understanding essential aspects of literary translation, a type of reported speech called *free indirect discourse* is taken as an example of the translation problems which successful literary MT systems would have to tackle.

1 Introduction

Over the last few years there has been an increasing number of studies that investigate the possibilities of using literature-specific MT systems in literary translation (see e.g. Lee 2011; Besacier 2014; Toral & Way 2015; Toral & Way 2018). As stimulating as these studies are, most of them do not discuss any narrative aspects of literary texts and therefore overlook an essential dimension of literary translation.

In this paper I argue that developing a successful literary MT system requires knowledge of the narrative structure of literary texts – as well as technological expertise, knowledge on translation workflows and readers' expectations. Being a specialist of (human) literary translation myself, my aim is to explain some basic aspects of narrative texts as well as their challenges in literary translation and that way hopefully feed into ethically responsible research on this topic.

In what follows I first define some key concepts that are necessary for understanding literary translation from a narratological point of view. Then I illustrate challenges that the developers of literary MT systems must address by discussing a particularly thorny question of literary translation: rendering *free indirect discourse* (henceforth FID, for a definition see below) in different languages.

2 Narratological Key Concepts for Literary Translation

The key concepts presented in this section come from classical, structuralist narratology that was designed to account for universal phenomena of narrative discourse regardless of cultural and historical context. In this sense structuralist narratology followed the pattern of structural linguistics that investigated the general rules and conventions of language (Steinby and Mäkikalli 2017, 9). Even though the representatives of classical narratology did not take into account changes that occur in the narrative structure when a text is translated, nor other aspects of translatedness (see e.g. Schiavi 1996; Tahir Gürçağlar, 2002) its key concepts offer a solid ground for observing narrative aspects in literary translation.

Steinby and Mäkikalli (2017, 10) point out that Gérard Genette's theory, presented in his seminal "Discours du récit" (in *Figures III*, 1972) became the essence of structuralist narratology thanks to the clarity and usability of his concepts. They write: "Although several of Genette's concepts, particularly focalization, voice, person, the status of the narrator, and the story-discourse distinction (--), have been the subject of extensive critical discussion, it is his conceptualization – with some additions, such as Wayne Booth's 'implied author' –

that forms the hard core not only of 'classical' narratology but also of more recent applications of narratology in other approaches to literary research." (Steinby and Mäkikalli 2017, 10) Owing to the centrality of Genette's notions and their usefulness in translation studies as well, the basic narratological concepts presented here are taken from his "Discours du récit" .

2.1 Story, Discourse and Narrating

Genette's (1972) theory is based on a fundamental division between three narrative levels which are interdependent, but all characterized by their own temporality (Scheffel et al. 2013, section 2). The first level is that of *story* (*histoire*), by which Genette (1972, 72) means narrative content, in other words "the events of the entire narrative in chronological and causal order prior to any verbalization thereof" (Mani 2013, section 3.1.). Naturally these events may not have had real existence, in which case they are inferred from *discourse* (*récit*) that is Genette's second level. For Genette (1972, 74) discourse is the only tangible level of narrative that can be the object of analysis. Discourse does not necessarily present the events in a chronological order and its time dimension is fixed by the text whereas the story-level time dimension is set in the narrated world (*diegesis*) (Scheffel et al. 2013, sections 3.1.1.–3.1.2.). Discourse is also the level where translation takes place and shifts on this level might have a repercussion on the two other levels. For instance, the fact that the first-person narration of *Robinson Crusoe* was shifted into third-person narration in some of the nineteenth-century German, Swedish and Finnish translations turned Crusoe from the narrator of the novel into a mere character (see Taivalkoski-Shilov 2015, 63). Genette's (1972, 72–73) third level is the narrating act itself (*narration*) and the situation where the *narrating* takes place (for instance Marcel relating his past life in *A la recherche du temps perdu*). The narrating should not be confused with the real-life composition of the fiction.

Some scholars, such as Meister (2005, 2011) have developed computer-based markup tools that tag and analyze temporal expressions in literary texts (Scheffel et al. 2013, section 3.2.3.4.). Such tools could turn out useful if they were integrated in literature-specific CAT tools. However, using them in fully automatic MT systems would yield low-quality translations because temporal expressions can have several functions in a literary text: for instance, tense variation is a marker of certain forms of reported speech in some languages (e.g. English and French).

2.2 Focalization

By creating the term focalization (*focalisation*) Genette wanted to distinguish two aspects of narrating that, according to him, had been hitherto mixed by several narratologists: narrative voice (who speaks?) and focus of narration (who sees?) (Genette 1972, 203–206). The notion of focalization is a means to answer to the question *whose point of view orients the narrative perspective*? Focalization designates the way narrative information is restricted in relation to the narrator, the characters and other possible entities in the storyworld (Niederhoff 2013, sections 1–2). Genette (1972, 206) divides focalization into three categories. In the case where the narrator knows more than the character(s) and relates this information to his audience (the so-called "omniscient narrator"), the focalization is zero. In the case where the narrator tells as much as the character knows, the focalization is internal. In the third case where the narrator shares less information than the character knows the focalization is external.

Focalization is a central concept for FID even though Genette later stressed that FID (belonging to the domain of who speaks?) and focalization (that answers to the question who sees?) should be distinguished from one another. As Kathy Mezei (1996, 70) points out, "(--) FID is frequently the mode by which a narrator focalizes through a character, appropriating that character's words to make the reader see through his/her eyes."

2.3 Reported Speech and FID

Reported speech or the way in which the discourse or the thoughts of literary characters are textually represented is an inherent part of narrative fiction. Genette (1972, 189–203) calls reported speech *récit de paroles*, which highlights the narrator's role as a mediator. The discourse and the thoughts of literary characters take place in the narrated world (the story-level) and even when characters seem to talk without the narrator's intervention, as in direct discourse (see below),[2] the narrator only pretends to give voice to the character (Genette 1972, 192).[3]

Reported speech appears in many forms ranging from a mention of a speech act to a direct quote that seems to reproduce also stylistically the character's speech (see Taivalkoski-Shilov 2010, 6–13). Types of reported speech can be located on a scale according to different criteria (see e.g. Genette 1972, 191–194; McHale 1978; Leech and Short 1981). For the purposes of this paper it suffices to distinguish between three basic types of reported discourse:

indirect discourse (e.g. Mrs. Smith **answered that she had not seen him that morning**.)

direct discourse (e.g. Mrs. Smith answered: **"No, I have not seen him this morning."**)

free indirect discourse (e.g. After Watson's question Mrs. Smith looked startled for a moment and then composed herself. **No, she had not seen him that** [or this] **morning**.)

The last type, FID, is a hybrid one. The range of its formal possibilities is extremely large (McHale 1978, 253). It is a combination of the narrator's and character's discourse that can appear in first-person or third-person narratives. Ordinarily it combines features of both indirect discourse (back-shift of tenses in retrospective narration) and direct discourse (deictic adverbs like "here" and "now", exclamation marks etc.). (Taivalkoski-Shilov 2006, 142.)

Genette (1972, 192) points out that one of the characteristic aspects of FID is its ambiguity. This is partly caused by the fact that FID is not dominated by a "higher clause" (McHale 1978, 253) and is not preceded by a reporting verb. That is why the interpretation that readers make of it depends on contextual cues and extra-linguistic phenomena (Tammi 2003, 43; Taivalkoski-Shilov 2006, 142). As Genette (1972, 192) observes, it is not always clear whether FID represents the character's speech or thought. Another ambiguity is between the narrator's and the character's voice; who is speaking, the narrator or the character? Furthermore, is the narrator empathetic or ironic towards the character? FID is sometimes also difficult to distinguish from *non-reporting narration*, which means the narration of other events than the speech of the characters (Taivalkoski-Shilov 2006, 137; Taivalkoski-Shilov 2010, 3).

2.4 FID as a translation problem

FID is a *translation problem* (Nord 1991, 151) that all translators irrespective of their level of competence and of the technical conditions of their work have to solve (Taivalkoski-Shilov 2006, 138). Research on the translation of FID shows that FID tends to shift into non-reporting narration, indirect and direct discourse or into other discourse types (Taivalkoski-Shilov 2006, 138–139). There are several possible explanations for this phenomenon. From the perspective of literary MT systems, the linguistic one is the most relevant. The challenge of translating FID is that its linguistic markers vary in different languages (see e.g. Kuusi 2003). Owing to differences in tense, pronoun, adverb and punctuation systems it tends to diminish or even disappear in translation. In some cases, this is because the indices of FID (for instance, the combination of a past tense verb with a present adverb) that are acceptable in one language are unacceptable or even ungrammatical in another. For example, the temporal systems of English and French are asymmetric (Poncharal 1998, 81–82, 241, 266): English uses the preterite tense (simple past) both for the narrator's discourse and FID, whereas modern French opposes the past used in narration (*le passé simple*) and the imperfect which is the typical tense for FID. Poncharal (1998, 180) concludes that in French there is a larger gap between the levels of story and discourse than in English. (Taivalkoski-Shilov 2006, 139.)

4. Concluding remarks

FID often leads to translation shifts in human translation. However, these shifts are probably more logical and less harmful for the narrative structure of the text than those caused by a MT system that is incapable of taking narrative aspects into account. Professional literary translators are capable of making shifts that cause least loss in translation and they can also compensate for the modifications they have to make to the narrative structure of the text. All this is so far lacking in MT systems.

[2] For the "reproductive fallacy" of direct discourse, see e.g. Sternberg 1981 and 1982, Rosier 1999, 237–244, and Taivalkoski-Shilov 2010, 7–11.

[3] For Genette the narrator's control over the character's discourse has its limits. According to him the character's voice substitutes for the narrator's voice in the case of free direct discourse, which he calls *discours immédiat* (Genette 1972, 194).

The problem with AI so far is that machine learning of narrative information requires considerable effort and has not been very successful. As Mani (2013, section 4) writes: "[In computational narratology] *Story understanding* systems (e.g. Wilensky 1978) never got very far, since (i) inferring characters' goals involves a large search space and the inferences may need to be revised during processing and (ii) humans use a great deal of knowledge to interpret even simple stories. Given Forster's exemplifying sentence " The king died and the queen died of grief," a child has no difficulty figuring out why the queen was upset, but imparting a body of such commonsense knowledge to a computer is difficult; (iii) aspects of language that are hard to formalize but that are important for story interpretation, such as humor, irony, and subtle lexical associations, have by and large eluded computational approaches."

References

Besacier, Laurent. 2014. Traduction automatisée d'une œuvre littéraire: Une étude pilote [Automatic translation of a literary work: A pilot study]. *21ème Traitement Automatique du Langage* Naturel, Marseille, 2014. P–T 1: 389–394. URL = http://www.aclweb.org/anthology/F14-2001

Genette, Gérard. 1972. Discours du récit : essai de méthode. *Figures III*. Éditions du Seuil, Paris, 65–282.

Kuusi, Päivi. 2003. Free indirect discourse in the translations of Jane Austen's novels into Finnish and Russian. In: Pekka Tammi and Hannu Tommola (eds.) *Linguistic and Literary Aspects of Free Indirect Discourse from a Typological Perspective*. Publications of the Department of Literature and Arts 6, University of Tampere, Tampere, 25–40.

Lee, Tong King. 2011. The death of the translator in machine translation: A bilingual poetry project. *Target: International Journal of Translation Studies*, 23(1): 92–112.

Leech, Geoffrey N. and Michael H. Short. 1981. *Style in Fiction: A Linguistic Introduction to English Fictional Prose*. Longman, London.

Mani, Inderjeet. 2013. Computational Narratology. Paragraph 9. In: Hühn, Peter et al. (eds.): *the living handbook of narratology*. Hamburg: Hamburg University. URL = http://www.lhn.uni-hamburg.de/article/computational-narratology

McHale, Brian. 1978. Free Indirect Discourse: a Survey of Recent Accounts. *Poetics and Theory of Literature* (3): 249–287.

Meister, Jan Christoph. 2005. Tagging Time in Prolog. The Temporality Effect Project. *Literary and Linguistic Computing* 20: 107–24.

Meister, Jan Christoph. 2011. The Temporality Effect: Towards a Process Model of Narrative Time Construction. In: Meister J. Ch. and W. Schernus (eds.). *Time. From Concept to Narrative Construct: A Reader*. de Gruyter, Berlin, 171–216.

Mezei, Kathy. 1996. Who Is Speaking Here? Free Indirect Discourse, Gender, and Authority in *Emma, Howards End* and *Mrs. Dalloway*. In: Kathy Mezei (ed.) *Ambiguous Discourse: Feminist Narratology and British Women Writers*. The University of North Carolina Press, 66 –92.

Niederhoff, Burkhard. 2013. Focalization, Paragraph 1. In: Hühn, Peter et al. (eds.): *the living handbook of narratology*. Hamburg: Hamburg University. URL = http://www.lhn.uni-hamburg.de/article/focalization

Nord, Christiane. 1991. *Text Analysis in Translation. Theory, Methodology, and Didactic Application of a Model for Translation-Oriented Text Analysis*. Rodopi, Amsterdam.

Poncharal, Bruno. 1998. *La représentation de paroles au discours indirect libre en anglais et en français*. Doctoral dissertation, University of Paris VII.

Rosier, Laurence. 1999. *Le discours rapporté: Histoire, théories, pratiques*. Duculot, Paris.

Scheffel, Michael, Antonius Weixler and Lukas Werner. 2013. Time. Paragraph 4. In: Hühn, Peter et al. (eds.): *the living handbook of narratology*. Hamburg: Hamburg University. URL = http://www.lhn.uni-hamburg.de/article/time

Schiavi, Giuliana. 1996. There is always a Teller in a Tale. *Target: International Journal of Translation Studies*, 8(1): 1–21.

Steinby, Liisa, and Aino Mäkikalli. 2017. Introduction: The Place of Narratology in the Historical Study of Eighteenth-Century Literature. In: Steinby Liisa and Aino Mäkikalli (eds.) *Narrative Concepts in the Study of Eighteenth-Century Literature*. Amsterdam University Press, Amsterdam, 7–37.

Sternberg, Meir. 1981. Polylingualism as Reality and Translation as Mimesis. *Poetics Today* 2(4): 221–239.

Sternberg, Meir. 1982. Proteus in Quotation-Land. Mimesis and the Forms of Reported Discourse. *Poetics Today* 3(2): 107–156.

Tahir Gürçağlar, Şehnaz. 2002. What Texts Don't Tell: The Uses of Paratexts in Translation Research. In: Hermans, Theo (ed.) *Crosscultural Transgressions.*

Research Models in Translation Studies II: Historical and Ideological Issues. St. Jerome Publishing, Manchester, 44–60.

Taivalkoski-Shilov, Kristiina. 2006. FID and Translational Progress: Comparing 18th-century and Recent Versions of Henry Fielding's Novels in French. In: Pekka Tammi and Hannu Tommola (eds.) *FREE language INDIRECT translation DISCOURSE narratology*: Linguistic, Translatological and Literary-Theoretical Encounters. Tampere university press, Tampere, 135−156.

Taivalkoski-Shilov, Kristiina. 2010 [1999] *When two become one*: Reported Discourse Viewed through a Translatological Perspective. In: ed. by Omid Azadibougar (ed.) *Translation Effects. Selected Papers of the CETRA Research Seminar in Translation Studies* 2009. URL = https://www.arts.kuleuven.be/cetra/papers/files/kristiina-taivalkoski-shilov-when-two-become-one.pdf

Taivalkoski-Shilov, Kristiina. 2015. Friday in Finnish: A Character's and (Re)translators' Voices in Six Finnish Retranslations of Daniel Defoe's *Robinson Crusoe*. *Target: International Journal of Translation Studies* 27(1): 58–74.

Tammi, Pekka. 2003. Risky Business: Probing the Borderlines of FID. Nabokov's *An affair of honor (Podlec)* as a test case. In: Pekka Tammi and Hannu Tommola (eds.) *Linguistic and Literary Aspects of Free Indirect Discourse from a Typological Perspective*. Publications of the Department of Literature and Arts 6, University of Tampere, Tampere, 41–54.

Toral, Antonio, and Andy Way. 2015. Machine-assisted translation of literary text: A case study. *Translation Spaces*, 4(2): 240–267.

Toral, Antonio, and Andy Way. 2018. What level of quality can neural machine translation attain on literary text? Chapter for the forthcoming book *Translation Quality Assessment: From Principles to Practice*. New York: Springer. Retrieved from: https://arxiv.org/abs/1801.04962v1

Wilensky, Robert W. 1978. Understanding Goal-based Stories. *Yale University Computer Science Research Report*.

When a 'sport' is a person and other issues for NMT of novels

Arda Tezcan, Joke Daems, Lieve Macken
LT[3], Language and Translation Technology Team
Ghent University
Belgium
firstname.lastname@ugent.be

Abstract

We report on a case study in which we assess the quality of Google's Neural Machine Translation system on the translation of Agatha Christie's novel *The Mysterious Affair at Styles* into Dutch. We annotated and classified all MT errors in the first chapter of the novel making use of the SCATE error taxonomy, which differentiates between fluency (well-formedness of the target language) and accuracy errors (correct transfer of source content). We modified the SCATE MT error taxonomy to be able to annotate text-level phenomena such as textual coherence (e.g. anaphora and coreference) and textual cohesion (e.g. lexical consistency) and literature-specific issues such as cultural references. Apart from annotating the errors in the MT output, we investigate how the machine translated version differs from the published human translated Dutch version of the book. We look at stylistic features such as lexical richness, cohesion, and syntactic equivalence.

1 Introduction

In literary translation, unlike in most other types of translation, the goal is not just to offer an adequate translation that preserves the meaning of the original, but rather to offer the reader a comparable reading experience (Toral and Way, 2015b). What makes this particularly difficult is the presence of cultural references (Besacier and Schwartz, 2015), the fact that literary texts are lexically richer than other texts (de Camargo, 2004) and the frequent use of idiomatic expressions. While, intuitively, these aspects make literary texts poor candidates for machine translation (MT), researchers have looked into the use of statistical MT (SMT) and, more recently, neural MT (NMT) for literary translation and found it to have a potential use. Still, as the research in this field is limited, "a thorough investigation of [MT's] utility in this space [...], both from the point of qualitative and quantitative evaluation" (Toral and Way, 2015b) is needed. Our goal with this study is to get a better understanding of raw NMT quality for literary translation by comparing the Dutch NMT translation of an English novel with its original Dutch translation. To the best of our knowledge, it is the first study into the usability of generic NMT for Dutch literary translation. We place particular emphasis on features that might impact the reading experience. In the following sections, we first highlight some of the relevant work that has been done on SMT and NMT for literary translation, we then discuss how we adapted the SCATE MT quality assessment approach to cover coherence issues relevant for the study of literary translation, followed by our analysis of the raw MT quality and a comparative analysis of key features (lexical richness, cohesion, and syntactic equivalence) between MT and the original human translation (HT).

2 Related research

Voigt and Jurafsky (2012) were some of the first to question whether statistical MT at the time was sufficiently developed to start thinking about using it for the translation of literary works, looking at Chinese to English translations. They were particularly interested in literary cohesion, and found literary texts to contain more dense reference chains (a higher number of mentions per entity) than non-literary texts. More importantly, they discovered that, while human translators manage to maintain this density, MT does not capture literary cohesion as well. If we are to apply MT to literature, they argue, we should think beyond the sentence level and incorporate discourse features in our analysis. Rather than looking at MT quality as such, Besacier and Schwartz (2015) studied the potential use of SMT for the post-editing of a literary text (an essay by Richard Powers from English into French). They found the process to be faster than manual translation would have been, and a group of readers found the product to be of acceptable quality. Still, Powers' official French translator found the post-edited product to be lacking in a few specific ways, such as source language structure being preserved in the target text, and cultural references or idiomatic language not being taken into account. Toral and Way (2015a; 2015b) looked into MT quality for literary translation by building a literature-specific MT systems for Spanish into Catalan, and French into English and Italian. Interestingly, they found that MT translation quality was comparable to human quality for 60% of the sentences (2015a), although they did work on closely related languages (Catalan and Spanish). Some of the main issues in the MT output were lexical choice, verbal tense, particles, and (gender) agreement (2015b).

MT quality improved even more in 2016, with the arrival of neural machine translation (NMT). Toral and Way (2018) argue that its increased quality (Junczys-Dowmunt, Dwojak, and Hoang, 2016) and the fact that NMT can handle lexically rich texts (Bentivogli et al., 2016) make it better suited for literary translation than SMT systems. By training an NMT and SMT system on literary texts and comparing the output, they indeed found that NMT quality outperformed SMT quality. Up to 34% of the NMT sentences were perceived to be of equal quality to human translations (compared to 20% for SMT). Professional translators, however, still preferred human translation over post-editing for literary texts (Moorkens et al., 2018), listing the following as the main limitations of MT: in literary translation, it is important to preserve the reading experience and in particular context is important, while MT has a fragmented view working on a sentence level; though NMT translates less literal than SMT, it is still not good with certain vocabulary and uses the wrong level of politeness; figurative language and cultural items remain difficult for both MT paradigms.

3 Method

3.1 Text selection

We use the Dutch MT translation of The Mysterious Affair at Styles, a 56000-word detective novel by Agatha Christie, as a case study. This book was specifically chosen as it is also the book used in the Ghent Eye-Tracking Corpus (GECO) (Cop et al., 2017), which contains eye movement data from Dutch speakers reading the human-translated version. As such, it offers a great reference for the reading process of manually translated literary text, which, in the future, can be compared to the reading process of MT. As the goal of literary translation is to preserve the reading experience, this will give us a way to establish which features in MT output (as discovered in this case study) have the greatest impact on said reading experience. In addition to this pragmatic choice, the novel contains key stylistic elements common to other literary works, which have been found to be potentially problematic for MT, such as the use of idioms, incomplete sentences in dialogue, and fragments in different languages, making our findings likely transferable to other literary works. The MT was generated by Google Translate (NMT), a freely available neural MT translation system, in May 2019.

3.2 Translation quality annotation process

To get an idea of the quality of neural MT for literary translation of English into Dutch, we first adapted the SCATE taxonomy (Tezcan et al., 2017) for literary translation, then annotated the first chapter of *The Mysterious Affair at Styles*. The SCATE taxonomy was selected because it was specifically developed to annotate MT output and it studies two distinct aspects of MT quality: fluency and accuracy. Fluency relates to all errors that can be spotted when looking at the target text only, such as grammar, lexicon, and orthography. The second aspect is accuracy, where source and target text are compared to discover potential issues such as omissions, additions, and mistranslations. As coherence was found to be such a crucial aspect of literary MT translation evaluation (Voigt and Jurafsky, 2012; Moorkens et al., 2018), we added a category 'coherence' for fluency. Subcategories were 'logical problem', if information made no sense when looking at the rest of the text, 'non-existing words' for words that did not exist in Dutch and as such made no sense, 'discourse marker', where a linking word expressed a strange relationship, 'co-reference', when there was a mismatch between entities that was not grammatically incorrect in the sentence itself, for example, a feminine pronoun referring to a male person mentioned in a previous sentence, 'inconsistency', when a term or notation was used inconsistently throughout the text, and 'verb tense', where the tense was grammatically correct, but it was illogical or wrong when compared to the rest of the sentence or surrounding sentences. In addition to coherence, we added a category for 'style & register', which consisted of the subcategories 'disfluency', for fragments or sentences that , though grammatically correct, were difficult to read or not quite idiomatic, 'repetition', when the same or a similar word is used more than once in a sentence, 'register', when the register (formal/informal) or regional variety did not match the target audience, and 'untranslated', where an English word for which a Dutch translation exists was left untranslated. An overview of the extended SCATE taxonomy can be seen in Figure 1.

FLUENCY

- coherence
  - logical problem
  - non-exisiting word
  - cultural reference
  - discourse marker
  - co-reference
  - inconsistency
  - verb tense
- lexicon
  - lexical choice
  - wrong preposition
- grammar & syntax
  - agreement
  - verb form
  - word order
  - extra word(s)
  - missing word(s)
- style & register
  - disfluency
  - repetition
  - register
  - untranslated
- spelling
- other

ACCURACY

- mistranslation
  - multiword
  - word sense
  - semantically unrelated
  - part-of-speech
  - partially translated
  - other
- do not translate
- untranslated
- addition
- omission
- capitalisation & punctuation
- other

Figure 1: Overview of the extended SCATE taxonomy.

We annotated the first chapter of the novel according to this extended SCATE error taxonomy using the web-based annotation tool WebAnno[1] (Yimam et al., 2013). The chapter is 351 sentences and 4358 words long, with an average sentence length of 11.5 words. Annotation was performed by one of the authors, who has over twenty years of experience in translation technology and translation quality evaluation. Fluency and accuracy were annotated in two distinct steps. For fluency, the annotator only had access to the target text, for adequacy, the annotator could compare source and target text. It is therefore possible for more than one annotation to be attached to the same word or phrase.

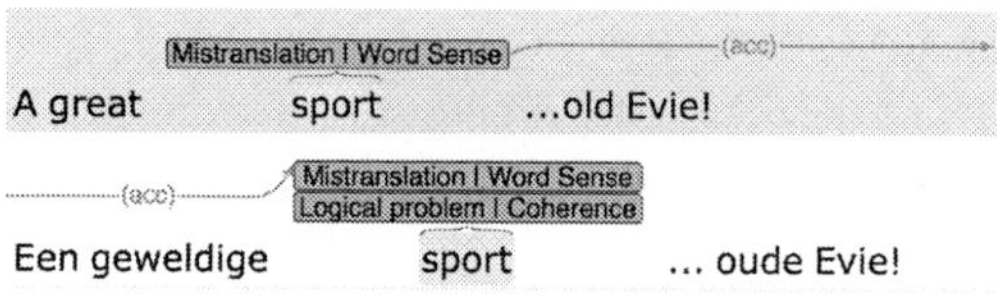

Figure 2: Annotation example.

An example of a double annotation can be seen in Figure 2. The English word 'sport' (in this context, a person), was translated in Dutch as 'sport' (an actual sport). From a fluency perspective, this is a logical problem, as the reader has no way of understanding why the word 'sport' would appear in this sentence. From an adequacy perspective, however, this word is a mistranslation of the type 'word sense', as the wrong sense of the word 'sport' was used here.

3.3 Textual feature analysis

In addition to the quality annotation of the first chapter, we compared some key textual features between MT and the original human translation of the novel. For these analyses, the entire novel was used.

As NMT is said to be able to handle lexically rich texts better than SMT (Bentivogli et al., 2016), we wanted to get an idea of the lexical richness of the novel and compare how well NMT manages to capture this richness as opposed to the original human translation. To do so, we look at the word frequency distribution, lexical density, and translation entropy.

To calculate lexical density, we used a variety of type-token ratio measures. The idea is that the more types there are in comparison to the number of tokens, the greater the lexical variety in a

[1] Version 3.4.5.

text. The following standard measures were used, where *t* is the number of types, and *n* is the number of tokens:

TTR (type-token ratio):

$$TTR = t/n \tag{1}$$

RTTR (root type-token ratio):

$$RTTR = t/\sqrt{n} \tag{2}$$

CTTR (corrected type-token ratio):

$$CTTR = t/\sqrt{(2n)} \tag{3}$$

A possible critique of the above formulas is that standard TTR-measures are sensitive to text length (Torruella and Capsada, 2013). We therefore also calculated Mass index and the mean segmental type-token ratio (MSTTR) as follows:

Mass index:

$$MASS = (\log(n) - \log(t))/\log^2(n) \tag{4}$$

MSTTR (Johnson, 1944): The text to be analysed is divided into equal segments of 100 words. MSTTR is calculated as the arithmetic mean of the TTR values for each segment.

Word translation entropy indicates the degree of uncertainty to choose a correct translation from a set of target words $t_i...t_n$, for a given source word s. If the probabilities are distributed equally over a large number of items, the word translation entropy is high and there is a large degree of uncertainty regarding the outcome of the translation process. If, however, the probability distribution falls unto just one or a few items, entropy is low and the certainty of target words to be chosen is high (Schaeffer et al., 2016).

Word translation entropy has often been analyzed as an indicator of cognitive effort in the context of human translation, by collecting translations for a given sentence from multiple translators (Carl et al., 2017; Vanroy et al., 2019a). In this study, however, we use it to measure average word translation entropy (AWTE) on document level, by making the calculation using all the words that appear in the source text and its translated versions, both automatically and manually. After calculating word translation entropy for each document pair (source-HT and source-MT), we take the arithmetic average of all entropy values to obtain AWTE.

For each unique source word s in the given source text, word translation entropy is defined as the sum over all observed word translation probabilities into target text words $t_i...t_n$, multiplied with their information content (Carl et al., 2017). For each source word s translation entropy is calculated as follows:

$$E(s) = \sum_{i=1}^{n} p(s \to t_i) * I(p(s \to t_i)) \tag{5}$$

where $p(s \to t_i)$ stands for the word translation probabilities of a source word s and its possible translations $t_i...tn$, which is calculated as the number of alignments $s \to t_i$ divided by the total number of observed translations $t_i...t_n$:

$$p(s \to t_i) = count(s \to t_i)/translations \tag{6}$$

The information I that is present in a distribution with equal probability of an event p can be formulated as in Equation (7).

$$I(p) = -\log_2(p) \tag{7}$$

While the probability p expresses the expectation for an event, the information I indicates the minimum amount of bits with which this expectation can be encoded.

In order to obtain translation options and calculate word translation probabilities, we used a freely available implementation of IBM models GIZA++ (Och and Ney, 2003) on source-HT and source-MT sentence pairs, respectively. While IBM-style models dominate the field of statistical word-alignment, they are also prone to overfitting the data and often propose many incorrect word alignments for rare words, a phenomenon called *garbage collection* (Moore, 2004). Furthermore, we can expect additional word alignment errors when this technique is used to align words between a source text and its machine translated version, which potentially contains translation errors. In order to be more confident about the differences between the AWTE values for HT and MT, we repeat the calculations by increasing the minimum frequency threshold for the set of source words we take into consideration. While a minimum threshold frequency of 1 covers all the source words in the source text (as each word occurs at least once), a threshold of n calculates AWTE only for the subset of source words that appear at least n times.

A key aspect of literary translation is the importance of cohesion (Voigt and Jurafsky, 2012) and looking beyond the sentence level (Moorkens et al., 2018). While the error annotation already covers cohesion, that analysis was limited to the first chapter and it is also very time-consuming. Inspired by previous work on local cohesion indices (McNamara et al., 2002; Crossley et al., 2016), we therefore measure local cohesion in terms of lexical and semantic overlap between a given sentence and the succeeding sentence(s) (up to two sentences). According to Crossley et al. (2016), looking at the lexical overlap between a sentence and the upcoming two sentences is a "significant indicator of perceived human text organization". While lexical overlap is measured by comparing lemmas of content words (nouns, verbs, adjectives and adverbs), semantic overlap uses WordNets in the NLTK package[2] and further compares the shared synsets (sets of cognitive synonyms each expressing a distinct concept) of content words. We report both the number of sentences that overlap with succeeding sentence(s) (with at least one overlapping lemma) and the total number of overlapping lemmas, summed over all sentences[3].

A final feature we studied was syntactic equivalence. One of the issues Besacier & Schwartz (2015) discovered for SMT was the fact that it followed the syntactic structure of the source text too closely. As we can expect NMT to translate less literal (Moorkens et al., 2018) and to lead to fewer word order issues than SMT (Bentivogli et al., 2016), the question is whether the syntactic structures found in the NMT output still closely resemble the source text structures or not.

As proposed by Vanroy et al. (2019b), we calculate syntactic equivalence between a source sentence and its translation in terms of their *cross value*, the number of times word-alignment links cross each other, averaged by the number of alignment links. Similar to Vanroy et al. (2019b), we calculate cross values in two ways: by looking at how (1) each individual word moves with respect to other words in the sentence, and (2) sequential words move together as a group. The second approach seeks the longest possible word sequence alignments between the source and target sentences with the following criteria:

- each word in the source sequence is aligned to at least one word in the target sequence and vice versa,
- each word in the source word sequence is only aligned to word(s) in the target word sequence and vice versa,
- none of the alignments between the source and target word sequences cross each other.

For both methods, we use GIZA++ to obtain word alignments between the source and target sentences automatically.

Vanroy et al. (2019b) argue that, cross value based on sequence alignments is a better representation of the clashing syntactic shifts that a source sentence has to go through to become the target sentence, as it indicates crossing groups of words rather than single entities. These two approaches are illustrated in Figure 3 for a source sentence in English and its translation in Dutch.

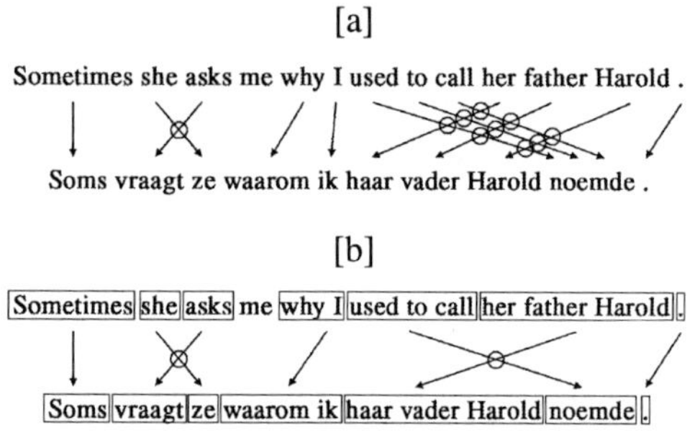

Figure 3: A visual representation of (a) word and (b) sequence alignments, and *crosses*, indicated by circles.

In these examples, each arrow indicates an alignment link between a source and target word or a word sequence. Please note that the source word "*me*" is not aligned to a target word in this example. In Figure 3a, we count ten *crosses*. This value is then averaged by the number of alignments to get average cross value of the whole sentence. In this case that is $10/12 = 0.8\overline{33}$. In Figure 3b, the cross value based on sequences is calculated as $2/7 = 0.286$.

4 Results

4.1 Quality

Looking at the NMT quality for the first chapter of the novel, we see that 44% of the sentences did not contain any errors. This is interesting in a number of ways. Firstly, earlier work comparing NMT to SMT and RBMT for English-Dutch general texts (newspaper articles and non-fiction) found that 33% of NMT sentences contained no errors (Van Brussel et al., 2018), which

[2] https://www.nltk.org/

[3] In a given sentence, each lemma is checked for overlap only once.

is lower than the 44% found here. Secondly, Toral & Way (2018) built a custom NMT system tailored to literary translation and found that up to 34% of sentences was perceived by native speakers as being of equal quality to a human translation, which is again lower. While 'not containing any errors' is in no way equal to 'comparable to human quality', this already gives some indication of the potential of NMT for the translation of literary texts from English into Dutch. As can be expected and as can be seen in Figure 4, performance decreases with sentence length. Most of the sentences without errors were shorter than 15 words. The maximum length for a sentence without errors was 37 words, which seems to align with findings that NMT quality decreases with sentence length (Bentivogli et al., 2016), to the extent that it might be outperformed by SMT for sentences longer than 40 words (Toral and Snchez-Cartagena, 2017).

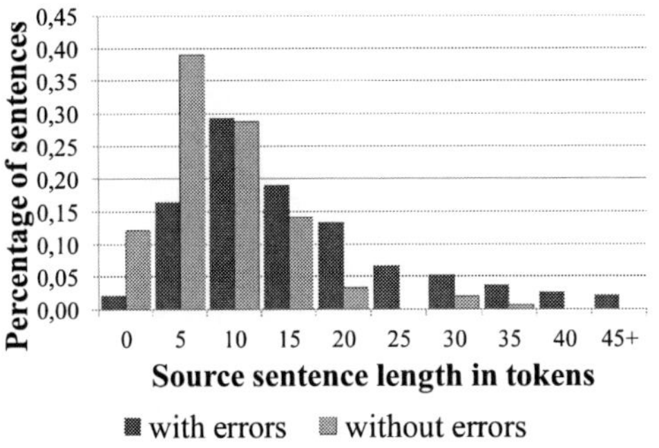

Figure 4: Distribution of sentences with and without errors per sentence length.

In total, 278 fluency errors and 205 accuracy errors were found in the dataset, which is in line with findings by Van Brussel et al. (2018) that NMT for English-Dutch contains more fluency issues than adequacy issues. Figure 5 shows how common the different subtypes are.

Coherence indeed seems to be a crucial addition to the taxonomy for literary translation, making up more than 50% of all fluency errors. Most coherence issues relate to logical problems. For accuracy, the most common error type is mistranslation, which makes up around 80% of all accuracy errors. Most mistranslation issues relate to multiword expressions, word sense issues, and issues without a specific subcategory. Style and register issues consisted mostly of disfluent sentences or constructions, indicating that this might still be an issue for NMT as it was for SMT (Besacier and

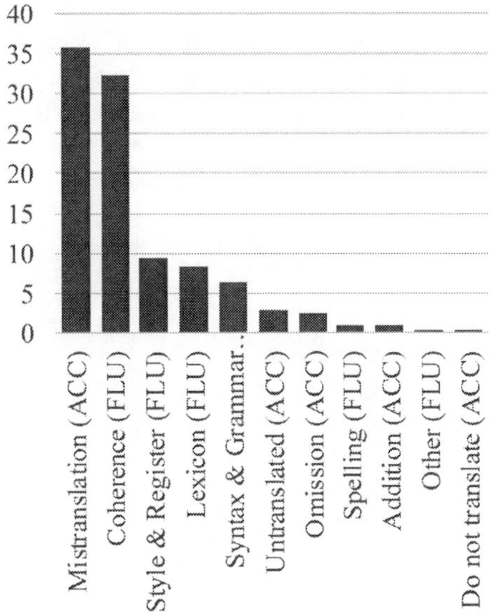

Figure 5: Frequency of error types expressed as percentage of all errors.

Schwartz, 2015). Issues found to be problematic in SMT by Toral and Way (2015b) such as lexical choice, verbal tense, and agreement, only occurred a few times in our NMT output, although it must be stressed that many cases of what we currently label as coherence issues might in other taxonomies be labeled as lexical choice issues. Indeed, Van Brussel et al. (2018) found lexical choice to be the most common fluency issue in Dutch NMT.

4.2 Key features

Lexical richness

Compared to the source text, both human translation and NMT have a higher number of unique words (5907 and 5948, respectively, as opposed to 5320 in the source). This difference is greatest for the number of singletons, i.e., words occurring only once, which is almost 500 words higher for HT and NMT as compared to the source. At first sight, this seems to indicate that both HT and NMT are lexically richer than the source text, with NMT the richer of the two. When comparing the number of unique words to the total number of words in Figure 6, this effect becomes even stronger: despite having the lowest number of total words, MT also has the highest number of unique words. A possible explanation for the higher number of unique words lies in the differences between both languages. In Dutch, compound nouns are often written as one word, whereas they consist of two words in English. For example, in Dutch, you can have the words 'eet' ('to eat'), 'kamer' ('room'), and the compound 'eetkamer' ('dining room') as three unique words, whereas in English there would be only two words: 'dining' and 'room'.

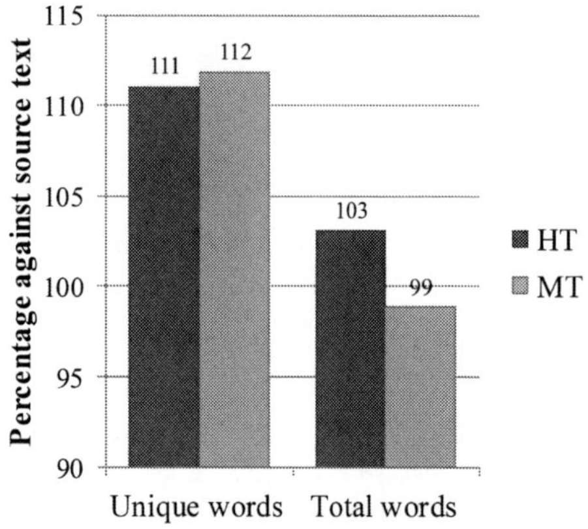

Figure 6: Unique words and total words as compared to the source text.

To further verify this claim, we studied lexical density by looking at a variety of type-token ratio measures, which we summarize in Table 1.

	Source	HT	MT
TTR	0.073	0.079	**0.083**
Root TTR	19.71	21.56	**22.17**
Corr. TTR	13.94	15.24	**15.68**
Mass index	**0.021**	0.020	0.020
MSTTR	0.648	**0.670**	0.660

Table 1: Summary of lexical density measures.

Most measures show comparable trends, with MT having a somewhat higher TTR than both the source text and the human translation. The measures for which this does not hold, however, are Mass index (highest in the source) and MSTTR (highest for HT), which have been argued to be better measures of lexical density than some of the other measures. As the differences between the three texts are rather small, we would argue that this seems to confirm that NMT can be at least as lexically rich as the original literary text and corresponding human translation. Still, in NMT, judging by the abundance of mistranslations and logical issues we found in the first chapter, it is possible that this lexical richness is in fact caused by translation errors. We therefore did not only look at the number of words in isolation, but we calculated translation entropy for HT and MT to gain a better understanding of what happens in translation. Figure 7 gives an overview of the translation entropy for words with different frequencies in the source text. It can be seen that translation entropy is always higher for HT, regardless of source word frequency.

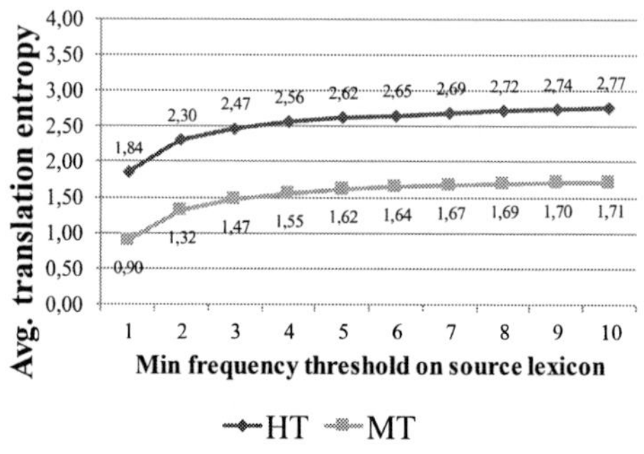

Figure 7: Average word translation entropy at different frequency thresholds.

This indicates that, in human translation, there is a higher level of uncertainty for the potential translations of a word than in MT, which, in turn, supports the theory that lexical richness in MT is potentially caused by erroneous translations, although a closer look at the data would be necessary to further substantiate that claim.

Cohesion

To study cohesion, we looked at the overlap of lemmas between a sentence and the following two sentences as these are a proxy for textual organisation, and we compare the overlap in the source text with that in HT and NMT for the number of sentences as well as the number of lemmas (as there can be more than one lemma overlapping in one sentence). Figure 8 shows lexical overlap (comparing lemmas of content words) and Figure 9 shows semantic overlap (comparing synonyms of lemmas of content words).

Looking at lexical overlap, it is clear that there is a greater level of overlap between sentences in the original than in either human translation or MT. The overlap for MT is somewhat higher than HT on a sentence level (a difference of 15 sentences), but quite a bit lower than HT on a lemma level (a differences of 92 lemmas). It is possible that English and Dutch have a different degree of lex-

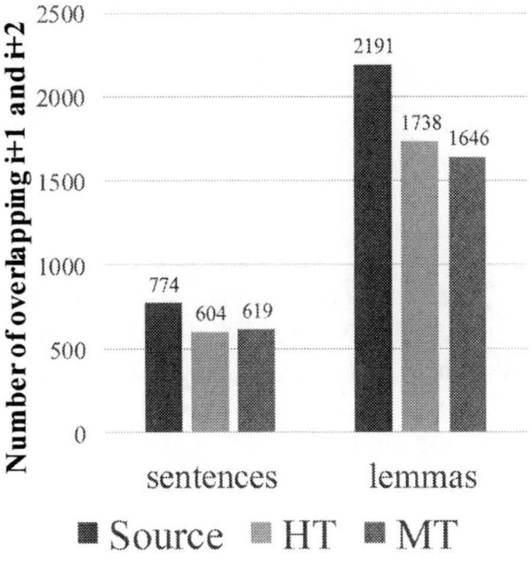

Figure 8: Local lexical cohesion.

ical richness, or this could also be caused by differences between original and translated text, with the latter generally exhibiting less variation than the first (Baker, 1996).

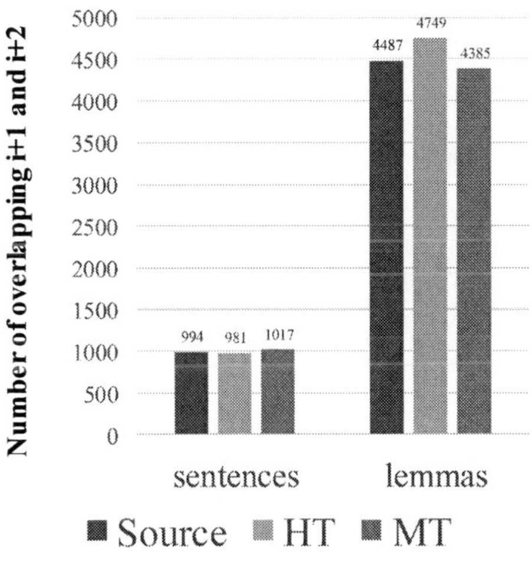

Figure 9: Local semantic cohesion.

Taking synonyms into account, the trend changes. On a sentence level, MT has a greater number of overlap than either the source text or HT (a difference of 23 sentences and 36 sentences, respectively), on a lemma level, HT has the greatest number of overlap (262 lemmas more than in the source, 364 lemmas more than in MT). A possible explanation, combining the information in Figure 8 and Figure 9, would be that, where the original author often reused the exact same word(s), the Dutch translator introduced synonyms more often. This is supported by research into literary translator style, where the avoidance of repetition in literary translation is considered to be a 'translation universal' (Ben-Ari, 1998). Looking at the number of exact or semantically-related overlapping lemmas, MT exhibits the least overlap. This could be an indication of MT being less coherent, possibly caused by errors in the MT output, as erroneous words would not be identified as semantically related. As for translation entropy, further analysis of the data would be needed to verify this.

Syntactic equivalence

Looking at syntactic variation between source and target text in Figurue 10, we clearly see that the cross values for human translation are much higher than those for MT. It is striking that 80% of all MT sentences have a cross value in the range $0 - 0.5$, indicating that MT follows the structure of the source text closely. The human translator introduced much more variation. There are 334 instances of cross values greater than 2.5 in human translation, compared to 16 in MT. The highest cross value for an MT sentence was 4, whereas for HT, there were 93 cases with a cross value over 4.

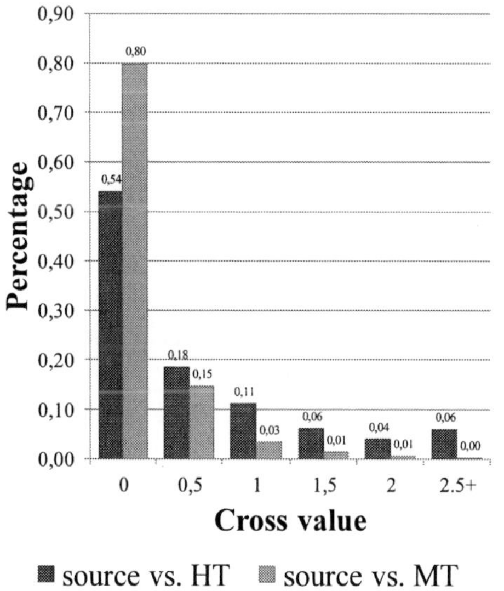

Figure 10: Frequency distribution of cross values (word).

Sequence cross values showed a very similar trend, with 78% of all sentences in MT having a cross value of zero, as compared to 52% in HT. This seems to indicate that the issue of MT closely following the source text structure leading to potentially unidiomatic language (Besacier and Schwartz, 2015) has not entirely been solved in NMT yet.

5 Conclusion

We conducted the very first case study into the potential of NMT for literary translation for the English–Dutch language pair. Our goal was to get an idea of the current quality of NMT for literary translation in this language pair and to identify likenesses and differences between source, HT, and MT for three key features: lexical richness, cohesion, and syntactic equivalence. In particular for shorter sentences, NMT quality seems promising. 44% of the sentences we studied contained no errors, which is impressive for a general-domain MT system. On the other hand, the MT output still contained many coherence issues and mistranslations. Despite MT containing the highest number of unique words, measures of lexical density did not confirm that it was lexically richer than the source text or HT. The higher translation entropy in HT further confirms that there is a difference between MT and HT, despite their TTR scores being comparable, a difference that might be caused by the many mistranslations found in the MT output. Looking at local cohesion, we found that it seems strongest in the source text, with human translation favouring synonyms over exact repetition and MT being the least cohesive of the three when considering overlapping lemmas. Our analysis of syntactic equivalence further shows that MT generally remains faithful to the source text structures, whereas HT shows a greater diversity compared to the source text. It remains to be seen to what extent these issues impact the quality of the output or the reading experience. Word order issues were rare in our dataset, but disfluency issues were more common. In the future, our goal is to annotate the rest of the novel and have a second independent annotator perform the same work, so we can compare the inter-annotator agreement and generate a gold standard annotation for the whole novel. We will then compare the textual feature analysis with the quality evaluation in more detail, to learn if and how they influence each other. This knowledge could then be applied to build quality estimation systems that use textual features as a proxy for quality. A second future goal is to use eyetracking to measure the readability of the raw MT output. As the GECO corpus contains information on the reading of the original English source and Dutch target text, we can use them as a reference to see to what extent MT impacts the reader's experience, and which features or errors impact this reading experience the most.

Acknowledgments

This study is part of the ArisToCAT project (Assessing The Comprehensibility of Automatic Translations), which is a four-year research project (2017-2020) funded by the Research Foundation – Flanders (FWO) – grant number G.0064.17N.

References

Baker, Mona 1996. Corpus-Based Translation Studies: The Challenges That Lie Ahead. In Harold Somers (ed.) *Terminology, LSP and Translation: Studies in Language Engineering in Honour of Juan C. Sager*, pp. 175-186.

Ben-Ari, Nitsa 1998. The Ambivalent Case of Repetitions in Literary Translation. Avoiding Repetitions: a "Universal" of Translation? *Meta*, 43(1), 68–78.

Bentivogli, Luisa, Arianna Bisazza, Mauro Cettolo, and Marcello Federico. 2016. Neural versus Phrase-Based Machine Translation Quality: a Case Study. In *Proceedings of the 2016 Conference on Empirical Methods in Natural Language Processing*, pp. 257–267.

Besacier, Laurent and Lane Schwartz. 2015. Automated translation of a literary work: a pilot study. In *Proceedings of NAACL-HLT Fourth Workshop on Computational Linguistics for Literature*, pp. 114–122.

Michael Carl, Srinivas Bangalore, and Moritz Schaeffer 2017. Why translation is difficult: A corpus-based study of non-literality in post-editing and from-scratch translation. *HERMES-Journal of Language and Communication in Business*, (56), 43-57.

Cop, Uschi, Nicolas Dirix, Denis Drieghe, and Wouter Duyck. 2017. Presenting GECO: An eyetracking corpus of monolingual and bilingual sentence reading. *Behavior research methods*, 49(2), 602–615.

Crossley, Scott A., Kristopher Kyle, and Danielle S. McNamara. The development and use of cohesive devices in L2 writing and their relations to judgments of essay quality. *Journal of Second Language Writing 32*: 1–16.

de Camargo, Diva Cardoso. 2004. An investigation of a literary translator's style in a novel written by Jorge Amado. *Intercâmbio. Revista do Programa de Estudos Pós-Graduados em Linguística Aplicada e Estudos da Linguagem*, ISSN 2237-759X, 13.

Johnson, Wendell. 1944. Studies in Language Behavior. *Psychological Monographs*, 56, 1.

Junczys-Dowmunt, Marcin, Tomasz Dwojak, and Hieu Hoang. 2016. Is neural machine translation ready for deployment? A case study on 30 translation directions. In *Proceedings of the Ninth International Workshop on Spoken Language Translation (IWSLT).*

McNamara, Danielle S., Arthur C. Graesser, Philip M. McCarthy, and Zhiqiang Cai. 2014. Automated evaluation of text and discourse with Coh-Metrix. *Cambridge University Press.*

Moore, Robert C. 2004. Improving IBM word alignment model 1. *In Proceedings of the 42nd Annual Meeting of the Association for Computational Linguistics (ACL-04)* pp. 518–525.

Moorkens, Joss, Antonio Toral, Sheila Castilho, and Andy Way. 2018. Translators' perceptions of literary post-editing using statistical and neural machine translation. *Translation Spaces*. 7(2), 240–262.

Och, Franz Josef and Hermann Ney. 2003. A Systematic Comparison of Various Statistical Alignment Models. *Computational Linguistics* volume 29, number 1, pp. 19–51.

Schaeffer, Moritz, Barbara Dragsted, Kristian Tangsgaard Hvelplund, Laura Winther Balling, and Michael Carl. 2016. Word translation entropy: Evidence of early target language activation during reading for translation. In *New directions in empirical translation process research*, pp. 183–210. Springer, Cham.

Tezcan, Arda, Véronique Hoste, and Lieve Macken. 2017. SCATE taxonomy and corpus of machine translation errors. In Gloria Corpas Pastor and Isabel Durán-Muñoz (Eds), *Trends in e-tools and resources for translators and interpreters*, pp. 219-244. Brill, Rodopi.

Torruella, Joan and Ramón Capsada. 2015. Lexical statistics and tipological structures: a measure of lexical richness. *Procedia-Social and Behavioral Sciences*, 95, 447–454.

Toral, Antonio and Victor M. Sánchez-Cartagena. 2017. A Multifaceted Evaluation of Neural versus Phrase-Based Machine Translation for 9 Language Directions. In *Proceedings of the 15th Conference of the European Chapter of the Association for Computational Linguistics (EACL), vol 1.*, pp. 1063–1073.

Toral, Antonio and Andy Way. 2015. Translating Literary Text between Related Languages using SMT. In *Proceedings of the Fourth Workshop on Computational Linguistics for Literature, NAACL*, pp. 123–132.

Toral, Antonio and Andy Way. 2015. Machine-assisted translation of literary text: A case study. *Translation Spaces*, 4(2): 240–267.

Toral, Antonio and Andy Way. 2015. What Level of Quality Can Neural Machine Translation Attain on Literary Text?. In J. Moorkens, S. Castilho, F. Gaspari, and S. Doherty (Eds.), *Translation Quality Assessment. Machine Translation: Technologies and Applications, vol 1.*, Springer, Cham.

Van Brussel, Laura, Arda Tezcan, and Lieve Macken. 2018. A fine-grained error analysis of NMT, PBMT and RBMT output for English-to-Dutch. In *Eleventh International Conference on Language Resources and Evaluation, European Language Resources Association (ELRA)*, pp. 3799-3804.

Vanroy, Bram, Orphée De Clercq and Lieve Macken. 2019a. Correlating process and product data to get an insight into translation difficulty. *Perspectives-studies in Translation Theory and Practice*, 1–18.

Vanroy, Bram, Arda Tezcan, and Lieve Macken. 2019b (*submitted*). Predicting syntactic equivalence between source and target sentences. *CLIN Journal.*

Voigt, Rob and Dan Jurafsky. 2012. Towards a literary machine translation: The role of referential cohesion. In *Proceedings of the NAACL-HLT 2012 Workshop on Computational Linguistics for Literature*, pp. 18-25.

Yimam, Seid Muhie, Iryna Gurevych, Richard Eckart de Castilho, and Chris Biemann. 2013. WebAnno: A flexible, web-based and visually supported system for distributed annotations. In *Proceedings of the 51st Annual Meeting of the Association for Computational Linguistics*: System Demonstrations, pp. 1-6.

Author Index

Association for Computational Linguistics
209 N. Eighth Street
Stroudsburg, Pennsylvania 18360

ISBN 978-1-5108-9251-4

CURRAN ASSOCIATES INC.
proceedings.com